How to **Get Published**

and make a lot of money!

SUSAN PAGE

How to Get Published

and make a lot of money!

PIATKUS

Dedicated with abundant gratitude to Sandra Dijkstra, my writing and publishing mentor and guardian angel extraordinaire

First published in the United States in 1997
by Broadway Books, a division of Bantam Doubleday Dell Publishing Group Inc.

First published in Great Britain in 1998 by
Judy Piatkus (Publishers) Limited
5 Windmill Street
London W1P 1HF

Reprinted 1998

The moral right of the author has been asserted

*A catalogue record of this book is available
from the British Library*

ISBN 0 7499 1841 1

Typeset by Phoenix Photosetting, Chatham, Kent
Printed and bound in Great Britain by
Mackays of Chatham PLC, Chatham, Kent

Contents

PART II TAMING THE MONSTERS
AND REAPING THE JOY

Acknowledgments

Literary agent Patti Breitman is the first person who encouraged me to turn my workshops into a book. It took several years for her seed to take root and sprout, but her little pep talks, and her spreading the word about my proposal in strategic places were critical to the final harvest.

My agent, Sandra Dijkstra, and my US editor at Broadway Books, Janet Goldstein, taught me a lot of what I share in these pages, and have been great working partners during this book's growing season. Janet's able associate, Betsy Thorpe, is efficient, resourceful, sympathetic, patient, and sunny – even on the cloudiest of days. We've enjoyed many laughs, and she has been a huge support.

An early and important mentor for me was my very first editor, Mindy Werner. She was wise, patient, and persistent with a beginner.

The vast experience of Berkeley editor and writing consultant, Dorothy Wall, filled gaps in my own information. For both fiction and non-fiction, she is a font of knowledge and skill, and I am very grateful for her help.

A big thank-you to Anita Goldstein, who supported me with research assistance, and whose expertise has been invaluable in helping to promote and market this book. My assistant, Alice Vdovin, is ever-ready with her on-going support for which I remain so grateful.

Ideas, facts, information-checking and support were contributed by the following people: Kevin Davis, David Garfinkel, Jeff Herman, Mark Oman, Nancy Peske, Bill and Elaine Petrocelli, Susan Schwartz and George Vdovin.

And as always, I couldn't write anything without the spiritual and material support of my warm, funny, and incredibly generous husband, Mayer.

Everything You Need to Know to Get Published Successfully in the Order You Need to Know It

Understand the Big Picture

Scene: A birthday party at a friend's home, 1988. My first book had just been published.

A young woman, Anne, approached me all excited about the chance to talk with a real author. She ebulliently explained that she had just received an offer for £3,000 from a well-known publishing house for her first book. After rejoicing with her, I began asking her a few questions. The conversation continued for an hour and a half, interrupted by various toasts, the cake and candles, and the present-opening. By the end of the evening, I had convinced Anne to turn down the offer, and to follow an alternative strategy which I outlined for her in detail.

Eight weeks and many phone calls later, she called to announce that she had just accepted an offer from a different house – for £35,000.

Having wandered around in the publishing wasteland for six years myself between the time I began writing my first book and the time I sold it, I understood why Anne had been doing almost everything wrong: she couldn't find out how to do it right, because straightforward information was nowhere to be found. Five writers had offered her five different strategies, based only on their own experiences. The books she consulted offered lots of background and explanations but never told her what she needed to *do*.

During my six years of confusion, hope and determination, I found that most of the time when I asked for information, I was inadvertently offering people a chance to vent their publishing horror stories. For years, I believed that there *is* no single way to get published, that even the people who succeed don't really know quite how they got there, and that all you can do is follow every suggestion that comes along, pray a lot, and hope you are one of the lucky ones.

Now it is eight years and four books later. I have learned what works, not only for me but for dozens of authors I've advised.

I've often read in job-search literature that people who get the jobs they want are not necessarily the people who are best qualified for those jobs; they are the people who knew how to get a job and who did all the right things. To a great extent, that principle applies in the publishing world too. To be sure, you have to have a good idea for a book and be able to present it well. But even if you have a superb book, you still have to do the right things in order to earn as much money as possible on the book, to have a smooth relationship with your publisher, and to support your book so that it achieves its full potential.

I've been taking notes for eight years now on every little nuance of the right things to do and the mistakes to avoid, and this book is the result. Part of its usefulness is that you will have information when you need it and not months later when someone you meet happens to tell you what you wish you had known much sooner.

THE STEPS IN BRIEF

Once you have an idea for a book, the basic stages from idea to publication are these:

Steps 1 to 4: Clarify your goals for the book and the book's distinctive identity, and start working on a fabulous title.

Step 5: Decide whether to self-publish or sell to a publisher.

Steps 6 to 8: Non-fiction: Write a proposal for the book, before *or* after you write the first draft of your manuscript. Fiction: Write your manuscript first. Then prepare a plot synopsis and proposal.

Step 9: Using your proposal, persuade a literary agent to represent you.

Steps 10 and 11: Let your agent sell the book to a publisher who will (usually) pay you an advance against royalties.

Steps 12 to 14: Write the book and work with your editor at the publishing house to refine it.

Steps 15 and 16: When the manuscript is complete, plan your promotion for the book.

Steps 17 to 20: Finally, the book will be published, and you will carry out your promotion plans.

Let me encourage you not to skip Steps 2 and 3 of this book in which I suggest you establish your goals for your book and give it a distinctive identity. No matter where you are in your process right now – whether you have just a few notes on a napkin or a full manuscript already – drop everything and spend the hour or two you will need to work through those two steps thoroughly. They will help you to make decisions all along the way and are critical to your ultimate success. I have seen writers proceeding without clarity in these two areas flounder and fail to attract the attention of an agent. When you are clear about your goals and your book's unique identity, success follows closely behind.

The time required for each step will vary greatly, of course, depending upon your circumstances. Exceptions and variations – both longer and shorter – are certainly common. But the following time line is typical:

Write the proposal	Six months
Locate and sign with an agent	Three months
Sell the book to a publisher	One to six months
Write the manuscript	Nine to eighteen months
Publication date	At least six to twelve month from acceptance of the final manuscript

THE ECSTASY AND THE AGONY

Both euphoric highs and crushing heartbreaks are extremely common among authors and would-be authors. You will probably experience your share of both, although my sincere hope is that the recommendations I've gathered together in this book will spare you the most common painful experiences and lead you directly to the highs!

The plain truth is, publishers do things that authors don't like. They change titles; they design ugly, unreadable jackets; they force you to alter cherished writing; they write flat, boring jacket copy and won't make changes you suggest; they withdraw promotion support or don't offer enough to begin with; they fail to get books broadly enough distributed; they don't print enough books to start with – and they may even become upset with you when you try to correct some of these problems yourself.

At times, publishers seem to operate on the general principle that authors know nothing about designing, producing or marketing books, and that if they are allowed to participate, they will waste valuable time and do more harm than good. They probably base this principle on thousands of episodes when it was true. So even if you do have excellent suggestions about the design, production and marketing of your own book, you have to pay for all the authors before you who were complete idiots and drove everyone at the publishing house to distraction.

Sometimes publishers have excellent reasons for doing what they do. But it can be very hard to understand why they take authors' preferences into account so little, since it is we who conceived of and wrote the manuscript, and we who must go out on the road and promote it. Ideally, publishing a book should be a full partnership. Many times, it is.

The real question you, as an author, must ask yourself is not, 'Might my publishers do something I don't like?' Most likely, somewhere along the way, they will. The question you want to ask instead is, 'How am I going to prepare myself to get the very most from my relationship with my publisher and to make it as productive and successful a partnership as possible?'

That is the question to which this book is the answer.

The short response is, work hard to write the best book you can; meet your deadlines; anticipate potential problem areas and do all you can to prevent them; and make yourself completely, totally easy to work with. Take initiative, ask for what you want, but *always* be cooperative and appreciative.

Of course there is another whole side to this story. Usually, publishers are completely wonderful. They do an enormous amount of work you don't even know how to do. They pour expertise, vast experience and gobs of money into your book. Most of the people you will work with are bright, delightful people who love what they do, have a great deal of respect for you and your work, and are genuinely excited about and invested in the success of your project. We may hear less about publisher/author collaborations that produce beautiful, quality books that are brilliantly marketed, because people who are hurt shout louder. But in fact, publishing houses are *deliberately* becoming increasingly author-friendly. Since they are always competing with each other for hot books, they do not want a reputation for disappointing their writers. Most authors are thrilled to be a part of this flourishing industry and have far more to celebrate than to regret. May this be the case for you!

WRITERS' CONFERENCES, COURSES AND WORKSHOPS

Because attending a writers' course or workshop doesn't fit tidily into my chronological outline but can be useful to you at any stage, I will mention it here.

Writers' conferences can be wonderful. They immerse you in the writing life, teach you valuable information about writing and publishing, put you in touch with other writers and give you the opportunity to connect with successful authors. They are perhaps most valuable for networking. Ask everyone you can for information about agents. (Be sure to read Step 9 first.) You will almost certainly meet several agents in person. It's possible you will be able to receive feedback on your actual writing.

Choose carefully the people you hang around with. These gatherings are filled with people who are anxious and insecure about their writing, as you may well be. As soon as you detect that someone is using you to feel better about him or herself, excuse yourself from the conversation. Don't let people brag and strut while you are feeling smaller and sicker inside. Find people who are supportive and want to connect with you on an equal footing. Most writers want to be genuinely helpful to each other.

You can find more information on conferences, courses and workshops in the Resources section at the end of this book.

PUBLICATIONS

There a number of specialist magazines offering support, encouragement and practical advice to published and unpublished writers. They cater for all interests – fiction and non-fiction – and most carry features on current aspects of writing and publishing. While you, as a writer, don't have to be fully informed about the inner workings of the publishing industry and all the latest gossip, these magazines do make you aware of market requirements. They also give details of forthcoming competitions, writers' conferences and other literary events. It's worthwhile tracking down copies of the magazines through libraries, friends or newsagents before taking out an often costly subscription – just to make sure the magazine in question has enough to offer you.

You'll find more details on Publications in the Resources section.

✳   ✳   ✳

Now, are you ready for a journey that may change your life? Like any other adventure, the only way to reach your destination is one step at a time. And the primary purpose of your goal is to enhance the quality of your efforts to reach it. In other words, it's all in the journey, so enjoy it to the max! Here we go.

Establish Clear Goals for Your Book

Time required: Thirty minutes now;
thirty minutes occasionally for review.

Why are you writing this book?

The answer to this question is important, because you will make different decisions throughout this project depending upon your true reason for undertaking it.

Are you writing this book

- because you have an important idea that deserves an audience or that will help people?
- because you have a burning desire to express your ideas or your story?
- because you love to write and you want to be rewarded for it?
- because friends have told you, 'You ought to write a book?'
- because you need a 'product' to sell when you give public presentations?
- because you want to position yourself in your marketplace and establish yourself as an expert in your field?
- because you want to make money?
- because you want to make your living as a writer?
- because _____?

What is your fondest hope for your book? Exactly what outcomes would you consider to be moderately or extremely successful?

I can't overemphasise the importance of *writing down* your goal or goals. In the first place, studies show that people who write down their goals are far more likely to achieve them than people who don't. But even more important, committing your goal to paper encourages you to be exact about it and forces you to face directly issues that may be vaguely uncomfortable for you. In your initial goal-writing attempt, you may not resolve such issues, but you will be doing yourself a great favour by raising the questions now so that you can be 'living them', as the poet Rilke says, and working toward a resolution as you go.

Be specific. If you want to make money, how much money? If you want visibility in your field, exactly how do you see that increased visibility happening? When do you hope to achieve your goal with this book? Is this particular project only one part of a bigger goal? How and when will the book fit into the big picture?

Be clear about whether writing a book is the right goal for you at this time. Would magazine articles or public speaking better meet your needs? Are you ready to write a book?

HOW CAN YOU KNOW WHAT ARE REALISTIC GOALS?

The secret to success in goal-setting is to keep your hopes high and your expectations realistic. This is an extremely difficult balance to achieve.

For example, let's say your fondest hope is that your book sells a million copies in hardcover and becomes a bestseller. You can see your title on the bestseller list. You have a clear vision of yourself in a comfy chair talking leisurely with Melvyn Bragg or Michael Parkinson on national TV.

Or let's say your hope is to receive excellent reviews for your book, especially in a specific publication. Maybe you would love to see your book on your local or regional bestseller list, or have it be widely accepted and used by people in your field.

You can't undo hopes like these. Nurture them. Reach for the stars! But at the same time, keep your *expectations* right down here on planet earth. Hope for all you want, plan for it, work toward it – but don't *expect* it to happen.

It's important to dream big because your vision, your hopes and dreams, will motivate you. If your hope is to sell 1,000 copies of your book, you will plan accordingly, and you are not likely to sell 30,000 copies. A limited vision will limit your potential.

But it is equally important to keep your expectations more limited *so that you can fully enjoy whatever success you achieve.* I have seen so many writers crushed when they achieved major success with a book – only because their expectations were inappropriately high.

If you expect £5 and you are paid £50, you will be elated. But if you expect £500 and you get £50, you will be crushed. It's the same £50; the difference in how you felt was because of your expectations.

Separating your hopes from your expectations may be a skill that is possible to learn only through painful experience. One of my clients was certain that his book would hit the bestseller list in the US. When it sold only 100,000 copies in hardcover (a major success by anybody's standards), he felt *disappointed!* He quite literally couldn't enjoy his success. He had allowed his hopes to become his expectations.

Don't let this happen to you. Keep your hopes high, but your expectations realistic. As spiritual writer Deepak Chopra says in *The Seven Spiritual Laws of Success*, 'Intention is desire with no attachment to the outcome.' Desire whatever you want, and let your desire motivate and inspire you and keep you excited. At the same time, graciously accept and *enjoy* whatever the outcome turns out to be.

It's not easy. But it is definitely the balance to strive for.

So, setting a goal for your book is hard because it is a mistake to aim too high or too low. What's a person to do?

Pick a goal that is just about in the middle. Let it be high enough to motivate you to do everything you can reasonably do for the success of your book. But let it be low enough so that there is an excellent possibility you can achieve it.

Or, as my friend Diane Ohlsson suggested to me, have freeze-dried goals. They will be a nice, reasonable size, but then when something auspicious happens to your book, you need only add water, and your goals will instantly grow larger as appropriate.

As you move further into the publishing process, and as you read more of this book, you will become more knowledgeable about what other books do and just what constitutes a middle goal for you. Modify your goal accordingly. After you sell the book, ask your editor what reasonable goals for your book would be. Talk to other writers. The more informed you can become, the more realistically you can set your goals.

I will now comment on two of the most common goals people have for their books.

IF YOUR GOAL IS TO EARN MONEY

The way you make money as an author is to sell your book to a reputable publisher. Vanity publishing and self-publishing (unless some sort of sponsor is involved) will invariably end up costing money rather than earning it (see Step 5).

Usually the publisher will pay you an advance against the royalties you will receive on the book as it actually sells to readers. The standard hardcover royalty scale is 10 per cent of the published price to 2,500 copies sold, 12½ per cent on the next 2,500 copies sold and 15 per cent thereafter. On mass market paperback sales the standard scale is 7½ per cent of the published price to 30,000 copies sold and 10 per cent thereafter.

If the royalty advance is small, say £3,000, you can reasonably expect to earn royalties beyond that as soon as the book's sales earn you that initial advance. If the royalty advance is large, say £20,000 plus, that could be the only money you will ever receive from that publisher for that book. You may be able to earn additional money from sales to foreign publishers and from other subsidiary rights. And, of course, if the book sells extremely well, you will eventually earn royalties over and above your advance.

I believe the most advantageous strategy for the author, most of the time, is to aim for the largest royalty advance possible. A large advance is money in your pocket – now. It may take a long time to see future royalties, because the book may be slow to sell. Also, the larger your advance, the more likely it is that your publisher will commit money to promoting your book after it is published.

There are exceptions to this general principle, especially for fiction writers. Sometimes, receiving less up front and delivering a magnificent manuscript can be more advantageous for your career in the long run than receiving a huge advance and delivering a book that falls short of the lofty vision a large advance implies. A huge advance might actually imperil your career if your book sells poorly. Here is where an agent's judgment and experience will be invaluable to you.

In general, however, in my experience, many authors make the mistake of setting goals for their books that are inappropriately low. Brand new to the field of publishing, they assume that, because they are unknown, they can't expect to make more than a few thousand pounds. But in fact, publishers have money, and you may be legitimately entitled to more of it up front than you think.

In Step 10, the sale of your book, I discuss the amount of royalty advances in detail. If one of your goals is to make money with your book, skip ahead and read that section before you make your first attempt at setting a specific financial goal for your book. Remember, as you proceed through these steps, you will review and revise your goals several times. To get started, do the best you can with the knowledge you have now.

IF YOUR GOAL IS TO MAKE A LIVING BY WRITING BOOKS

Don't quit your day job the moment you sell your first proposal. It is the rare person who makes a living by doing nothing but writing books.

There are a few ways to do it if you are talented and dedicated:

1. Be an extremely successful fiction writer.
2. Become an entrepreneur, self-publish your books, and find ingenious ways to market them. This is a full-time and risky endeavour.
3. Find a niche, and keep turning out books at the rate of about one a year. Each book has to be at least moderately successful, so the publisher will continue to pay you an advance equivalent to a decent salary for each book.

    Niches like this are hard to find. Examples might be a series of specialised cookbooks, cartoon books, books of aphorisms or quotations, a series of books on any topic of wide interest such as gardening or sailing, business books, or any books that sell because of your particular personality.

    An example of a niche writer is Dianna Booher who has written over twenty-five books on business topics such as *Communicate with Confidence!* and *Send Me a Memo*. But even Dianna doesn't write exclusively; she is also a professional speaker.
4. Write a blockbuster non-fiction bestseller.

    There are probably a few people in the history of publishing who have made enough money on one book – and then several follow-up books – that they can literally retire and live off their royalties: people like Scott Peck, John Gray and the *Chicken Soup for the Soul* authors, Jack Canfield and Mark Victor Hansen.

    Most books that appear on the bestseller list probably earn from £50,000 to £300,000 for their authors. That's before the agent's percentage and taxes. It's a tidy sum. It may give you a year's sabbatical, but it probably won't pay your mortgage for the rest of your life.

Besides, getting on to the bestseller list is truly rare. In 1997 an average of 83,000 different titles passed through the tills of general High Street bookshop outlets in the UK – only 5,000 of which accounted for more than half of the total sales generated. And the vast majority of those 5,000 titles never made it on to the bestseller lists. You figure out the odds.

The vast majority of bestsellers are by people who are already rich or famous or both. On any given week, you will see that most of the non-fiction bestsellers are by celebrities. The authors who aren't famous are probably rich. Harvey Mackay devoted a year or more of his life and huge sums of his own money to make *Swim with the Sharks Without Being Eaten Alive* into a bestseller. The same is true for the authors of *Chicken Soup for the Soul*, Mark Victor Hansen and Jack Canfield. They already had several staff people working for them, and they invested large sums in promoting their books. Jack told me he pays one person full-time just to get the books listed in a variety of catalogues!

Of course, you don't have to get onto the bestseller list in order to make good money from your books. A great many books earn £50,000 or so, even though they may never appear on even a regional bestseller list. But how often can you turn out a £50,000 book? And how many £50,000 books can you write in a row?

In short, very few people make a living by writing books alone. Browse through the section of your bookshop that will carry your book when it is published. Most of the authors, you will discover, are actively engaged in some pursuit besides writing. They are professors, economists, journalists, therapists, celebrities, professional speakers, entrepreneurs or corporate executives. They are actively engaged in whatever field they are writing about. In addition, they have probably spent a great deal of time and money promoting their books.

Far be it from me to discourage you from becoming a full-time book writer if that is your goal. You may be able to make your book or books one component of a business based on your area of expertise. But you will probably also need to offer consulting, workshops or direct services in addition to your writing. If you become well-known for your presentations about consumer fraud or diversity in the workplace, you can make money from your speeches and your books, and they will promote each other. If you are looking to writing books as a way to change your lifestyle, consider writing combined with downshifting in your current career.

Start slowly. Learn as you go. But keep a source of income until you see clearly what you are going to be able to do on a long-term basis with your books.

EXERCISE: SETTING GOALS

Do this exercise as best you can with the information you have now. Return to it periodically and revise it as you learn more.

1. Complete this sentence: I am writing this book in order to

_____.

Complete the next two sentences by listing your goals for the number of books sold by a certain date, total amount earned, amount of royalty advance, type and amount of visibility the book gives you, or what ever other measures are appropriate for you. Be specific and detailed.

2. My highest dreams for this book are _____
_____.

3. A realistic expectation for this book is _____
_____.

Now, select a goal or goals that are high enough to motivate you to achieve the full potential of your book, and low enough that you can reasonably expect to achieve them.

4. My goal(s) for this book (is, are) _____
_____.

Establish Your Book's Unique Identity

Time required: Sixty to ninety minutes now;
thirty minutes periodically to revise.
(Possibly the most important sixty minutes of your writing career.)

For your book to succeed, it must make an original contribution. Agents and editors will not consider one more legal thriller, one more serial killer novel, one more book on what's wrong with British business, or one more low-fat cookbook – unless it truly contains a new angle.

If you have an unusual personal experience that will interest others, new information about a historical figure, an innovative plot for a mystery, or you can fill a genuine gap in the existing literature, this is ideal.

For example, my second book, *Eight Essential Traits of Couples Who Thrive*, was motivated by my observation that most books about couples are written by therapists who worked almost exclusively with couples who are unhappy or dysfunctional. I felt the need for a book that looked at healthy, happy marriages to see what we could learn from them about how to make love work. My new angle was to write a book about healthy rather than dysfunctional relationships.

But not every new book contains brand-new ideas. Your book may be based on known material and can still be distinctive in its presentation, its vocabulary or its imagery. Instead of writing one more software manual, IDG Books capitalised in America on people's fondness for playing dumb about computers and called its series *The Internet for Dummies*, *Windows for Dummies*, and so on. It became a worldwide success. Jay Conrad Levinson used the idea of non-establishment, underground approaches with his book, *Guerrilla Marketing*. Now there is a whole series of Guerrilla books on many aspects of business. Or instead of *How to Negotiate*, Joel Edelman wrote *The Tao of Negotiation*, a title that conjures up a scene of calm, spiritually mature people in a room together, working things out. These are all examples of creative imagery and vocabulary.

There is no end to the novel ideas (!) that can give your work of fiction a distinctive twist. Can you put your thriller plot idea in a historical setting? *The Celestine Prophecy*, for example, rather than presenting New Age philosophy in a standard non-fiction format used an Indiana Jones–type plot to introduce the ideas, blurring the line between fiction and non-fiction.

Perhaps your original contribution is that you organise information in a novel way, or make it more accessible to the reader than any previous book has. The more dramatically innovative you can be, the easier it will be for you to gain the attention of agents and editors – and ultimately the attention of booksellers and book buyers.

So, *whatever* stage your book is in now, stop everything else and answer the questions below. Be sure to review and revise them periodically. You may find as you get into your writing that the distinctive angle will actually change or become more obvious, or that you have found far more compelling words with which to convey it.

If you aren't sure how your book is distinctive, this exercise will motivate you to begin thinking along these lines. Spend a little time with the exercise now to prime the pump. As you work, if you are on the lookout for them, distinctive angles will occur to you and may even alter the direction of your work.

EXERCISE: DEFINING YOUR BOOK'S DISTINCTIVE ANGLE

Important Note: You will actually use all of the material in this exercise in the writing of your proposal. When you get to that step, you will be grateful to have completed this homework now. Complete all four steps, even though they may seem similar.

1. Pretend a potential literary agent has just asked you, 'How is your book different from all the other books on this topic?' Write down one or two sentences that give a succinct, dazzling answer to the question. (Keep returning to these sentences as you write until you hone them to perfection.)

2. Pretend you are about to appear on a national TV show to talk about your book. Prepare both a five-second and a fifteen-second promotional spot, designed to run the day before, that will make your show irresistible to viewers. You know, the kind that ends with, '. . . tomorrow on *This Morning with Richard and Judy.'*

3. Pretend you are the sales rep for your publisher. You are trying to persuade a bookshop to carry your book, but because you represent so many other books also, you have only thirty seconds to convince a bookseller. Write out your thirty-second sales pitch.

4. Write a paragraph with the following outline:

   A. Why is there a need for your book? For example, what pain are readers experiencing in their lives? What information do they lack? What predicament exists in society? What vacuum is longing to be filled? In what new way could readers be entertained? What's the problem? Where's the void?

   B. How will your book fill this need, resolve this pain, supply this information, explain this predicament, fill this vacuum, provide this entertainment or solve this problem?

   C. Why are you the person who should write this book? What experiences in your life qualify you? How did you gain your expertise or your special knowledge?

   Again, make one attempt to answer these questions now, and keep returning to them as your ideas become sharper.

Start Working on a Fabulous Title

*Time required: Thirty minutes now;
thirty minutes periodically.*

A spectacular title can add focus, energy and excitement to your book project in its early phases. The *process* of title-searching may help you to zero in on your book's most distinctive features. And of course, a compelling title is a critical tool for marketing your book later on. So it is a good idea to start the search for a great title early in your process.

Often, coming up with the perfect title is difficult. It is a part of the process over which you have somewhat less control, because you are dependent upon inspiration.

So start looking for a fabulous title now. And get your friends and family and co-workers in on the process. Here is a job where collective inspiration works extremely well.

Common wisdom is that when you find the perfect title, you will know it instantly. In my experience, this is true sometimes but not always. It may take you a while to realise that you have blundered into brilliance; one title will slowly begin to separate itself from all the others.

CHARACTERISTICS OF A GOOD TITLE

A title must accomplish several tasks. Ideally, it will

- instantly say what the book is about.
- pique our curiosity.
- be distinctive.
- be memorable.
- be positive.
- feel on target, exciting, and compelling *to the author.*

Often, the title you start out with will meet the first requirement, but that's all. My first title for *If I'm So Wonderful, Why Am I Still Single?* was *How to Find Love: A Guide for Singles*. (Yawn.) It's not distinctive or memorable.

Some titles meet several of the criteria, but they are negative instead of positive. Don't call your book, *Stop Losing Money in the Stock Market*. Instead call it *How to Get Rich Overnight*.

Probably the least effective titles are simple labels that say, 'This is the subject matter you will find in this book.' For example,

Marriage and Families
The Art and Practice of Loving
Anger and Forgiveness

However, sometimes the subject matter you are 'labelling' is interesting enough that a label is all you need:

The 7 Habits of Highly Effective People
Women Who Love Too Much
The Aquarian Conspiracy
Raising Your Spirited Child

What can a title do besides label a book's topic? It can

- introduce a new, intriguing term

Passages
Megatrends
The Enneagram Made Easy

- make an irresistible promise

Positively Outrageous Service
Wealth Without Risk
Eat More, Weigh Less

- tell you in a nutshell the basic premise of the book; give away the secret in the title

Lies My Teacher Told Me
Smart Women, Foolish Choices
The Overworked American
Men Are from Mars; Women Are from Venus

- conjure up an image; introduce a powerful metaphor

The Silence of the Lambs
Swim with the Sharks Without Being Eaten Alive
The Bridges of Madison County

- ask a question or make a statement that people ask or say all the time in real life

If I'm So Wonderful, Why Am I Still Single?
I Never Promised You a Rose Garden

In addition to examining the *function* of a title, you can also seek inspiration by looking at title *patterns*. For example:

- Blank and Blank

The Chalice and the Blade
War and Peace

- A statement

All I Ever Needed to Know I Learned in Kindergarten
Love Is a Verb

- A question

Why Do I Think I Am Nothing Without a Man?
How Could You Do That?
Who Put the Butter in Butterfly?

- An oxymoron or words used in unusual combinations

Emotional Intelligence
Simple Abundance
Intimate Strangers
Steel Magnolias
Necessary Losses

- A specific number of laws, rules or guidelines

The Seven Spiritual Laws of Success
The 7 Habits of Highly Successful People
Eight Essential Traits of Couples Who Thrive

- A new idea with a simple explanation after a colon

The Transcendent Child: Tales of Triumph Over the Past

- A single word

Passages
Chaos

- Blank who . . .

Women Who Love Too Much
Men Who Can't Love

- A variation on a classic title, literary or Biblical reference

My Old Man and the Sea
The Cinderella Complex
The Road Less Travelled
For Whom the Bell Tolls

- Two closely related topics beginning with the same word

Our Bodies, Ourselves
My Mother, Myself
Women's Bodies, Women's Wisdom

- Alarming, shocking words or concepts

Future Shock
The Population Bomb
Silent Spring

- Words with dual meanings

Lying on the Couch

- And of course, good old How To . . .

How to Talk So Kids Will Listen and Listen So Kids Will Talk
How to Be Happier Day by Day

Books in Print contains more than 6,000 titles that begin with the words 'How To'. The phrase may be overused, but that is probably because it continues to be effective. 'How to' sounds boring until it is followed by something people really want: How to Be Irresistible to the Opposite Sex, for example.

Marketing copywriter David Garfinkel reminds his students that 'How To' must be followed by the *result* you will provide people with, not the ways you provide the result. Notice that Dale Carnegie named his book *How to Win Friends and Influence People*, not *How to Improve Your Listening Skills and Learn to Remember People's Names*.

Remember that bookshops will be looking up the title of your book on a computer for inquiring customers, so avoid words that can be spelled in different ways or that could easily be either one word or two. And don't make your title too hard for people to remember. The title of Jeffrey Mayer's helpful book on getting organised is clever and communicates a point. You can remember the point, but the exact title is hard to recall: *If You Haven't Got the Time to Do It Right, When Will You Find the Time to Do It Over?*

What about subtitles? Subtitles are wonderful because they give you a second chance to interest a potential buyer. You can add more information in a subtitle or suggest exactly how the book will help the reader. But remember, in many situations, the subtitle will not be used: when a chat show host is announcing the title of your book, for example, or when it is being listed along with other books in an article – or a bestseller list!

So the title has to do most of the work. With rare exceptions, the title itself should convey what the book is about and why the public should be interested in reading it.

Good luck with your title. Maybe you already have a super one. If not, it can be a true challenge to find one that tells exactly what your book is about and how it is distinctive; that stands out from the pack; and that is clever, memorable and irresistible.

HOW TO FIND THE PERFECT TITLE

As experts on creativity tell us, inspiration often comes as a result of four steps. First you have to do your homework: Think about the function and pattern of your title as suggested above. Conduct some of the activities I'm about to suggest. Work at it for a while. For the second step, let go of the whole thing. Relax and forget about it. The seeds you have planted by doing your homework are gestating.

The third stage is the *aha!*, when the answer you were looking for magically appears in your brain while you are in the shower or in a conversation with a friend. And the final stage is testing your idea in the real world. Try it out on people and check their reactions. Live with it yourself for a while. Measure it against the criteria discussed above.

In searching for titles myself, I find I move through all these stages numerous times. Brilliant titles emerge within me in the dark of night, only to reveal themselves as fatally flawed when seen in the light of day. So I go back to working at it and then letting go of it in a hopeful rhythm that continues until someone – in my case, usually not I – comes up with the perfect solution that does stand the test of time.

Here are some activities that will stimulate your creativity. Remember, each exercise you play around with will indirectly help to get you to your final title, even if it doesn't produce the title instantly, because all these activities will feed your creative centre. In the end, you have to rely on good ol' inspiration, yours or someone else's.

BROWSE IN BOOKSHOPS

With pad in hand, list titles that grab you. Note the pattern and function of each title.

Then, take your list home and invent titles for your own book that copy a variety of patterns and functions you have discovered.

HOLD A FORMAL BRAINSTORMING SESSION
WITH FRIENDS AND FAMILY

Invite your most lively, creative friends over, and cook them a meal in exchange for forty minutes of their time. Brainstorming works well with as few as three or as many as ten or fifteen people. It's a lot of fun too. But it is important to follow these rules:

Select a recorder who will write all the suggested titles down as they come flying. Ideally, it will be on a blackboard or flip chart so everyone can see what has been suggested so far.

Brainstormers should be encouraged not to censor their ideas. Every suggestion is welcome, however zany or improbable, and even if it copies a famous title or it has been done before. You never know what lousy or silly idea is going to trigger the perfect idea in someone else.

Absolutely no judgments or criticisms are allowed during the brainstorming session. No one can say, 'That won't work,' or 'But it doesn't say what the book is about.' All those evaluations can come later when you go over the list. No discussion is allowed during brainstorming, nothing to distract people from thinking up titles.

At the end of the session, you may want to go back over the list and let brainstormers vote for their top five favourites. But it is you who will ponder the list later to see whether your ideal title has appeared, whether some titles give you the idea you were searching for, or whether you have to keep looking.

Brainstorming is successful when you come out of a session with ideas that no single person had going into the session. The process itself, as opposed to any one person, actually produces the ideas.

HOLD A PRIVATE BRAINSTORMING SESSION

Force yourself to write down thirty titles in one sitting. Not twenty-eight. Not twenty-five. It has to be thirty. Sometimes it is those final titles you have to struggle for that turn out to hold the key to success.

SEED YOUR DREAMS

Before you go to sleep, do a little ritual to ask your dreams for help. Write your request on a slip of paper and put it under your pillow. Or light a candle and ask your dream muse to assist you. Then, in the morning, as soon as you wake up, write down everything you can remember. Do this for a full week, or several times in one week.

PUT OUT THE WORD THAT YOU ARE LOOKING FOR SUGGESTIONS

Don't overlook this all-important, easy strategy. Your friends are probably excited about your book project and will be thrilled to help you. Some people really enjoy a challenge like this and will have a good time with it, calling you every few days with new titles.

You might even put the word out on the Internet, as long as you don't give away the distinctive qualities about your book.

OFFER AN AWARD FOR THE PERFECT TITLE

If you make your award appealing enough, you may get several people working very hard to help you solve your problem.

✳   ✳   ✳

As we said, the perfect title can enhance your motivation, focus and excitement, and can make an enormous difference to the sales figures for your book. Start the process of title searching early, and keep working on it as you go.

Decide Whether You Are Going to Self-Publish or Sell to a Publisher

*Time required: One to fifteen hours of
research and decision-making.*

SELF-PUBLISH OR SELL?

Very few authors choose to self-publish, many preferring to make the most of the knowledge and expertise of the publishing houses. But this is an option which is open to you and may be worth considering. You should be aware, however, that the chances of being highly successful, if you publish in this way, are very small.

So what are the advantages and disadvantages of self-publishing compared to selling to a publishing house?

There are two significant differences:

1. When you self-publish, you have to shell out a considerable amount of money up front. When you work with a publisher, you usually *receive* money up front.
2. When you self-publish, you have to manage your project by yourself or pay a self-publishing service to manage it for you. This simply means you have to do more of the work yourself. You must not only write your book, but also get it edited, copyedited, designed, printed, distributed, marketed and promoted. All of this takes time and money.

Successful self-publishers are entrepreneurs. They enjoy taking risks. They start a small business and devote themselves full-time to marketing their books. The actual writing is a small part of what they do. If your true passion is *writing*, self-publishing may not be for you.

Even if you don't do it full time, to be successful at self-publishing you must either (a) enjoy managing and marketing; or (b) have enough money to pay someone else to manage and market for you (though a stand-in will rarely do as good a job as you would do yourself; usually the person you hire will be managing other books too); *and* (c) have an almost automatic, easy way to sell large numbers of books. For example, you may be a professional speaker who can sell books at your own presentations, or your book may have an extremely targeted, easy-to-reach audience.

If you fit the above criteria, you may wish to consider self-publishing for the following reasons:

1. You maintain total control over the design, the content, the title and the cover of your book. As we'll see, authors who sell their books to established houses sometimes have to fight over these elements, and may be forced to sacrifice cherished desires.
2. You can zoom your book into the marketplace much faster than a publishing house can. A month or two after you have completed your writing, your book can be on sale. By contrast, publishing houses have long production and marketing schedules that require at least six to twelve months between the completion of the manuscript and the finished product, sometimes longer.
3. You can make more money, faster, even with fewer total sales than an author who sells to a publishing house. This is because, even after the cost of producing and marketing the book is deducted, more of the profit will be going directly into your pocket. Publishers, on the other hand, will pay you only a small percentage of the proceeds – and if you have an agent, he or she will have to receive a percentage of the proceeds as well.

   When you self-publish, you may put, say, £5 into your own pocket for each copy you sell of a £15 hardcover. If you sell only 1,000 copies, you've got £5,000; if you sell 5,000 copies, which isn't that many as books go, you've got £25,000. With a good, strong book and lots of marketing skill, higher sales even than this may not be difficult to achieve.

   Were you to sell this same book to a publisher, your contract might give you something like £1.50 per book. Now, to earn £5,000, you have to sell 3,300 books; to earn £25,000, you have to sell more than 16,000 books, not 5,000. Not very many books achieve that level of sale.
4. If you were unsuccessful the first time you tried to secure an agent and sell your book, self-publishing can be a stepping stone to

mainstream publishing. If your self-published book sells a lot of copies in its first year, you will be in a stronger position to approach an agent.

The advantages of selling your book to a publisher, by contrast, are these:

1. You will usually be paid to write your book.
2. Your publisher will manage many of the details of producing, distributing and marketing your book, thereby saving you vast amounts of effort, time (including the often slow learning curve of self-publishing) and up-front capital.
3. You will be working with a variety of experienced professionals including your agent, and your publisher's editorial, publicity, marketing and sales departments. While you may at times feel constrained or frustrated by their traditions and protocols, you will benefit enormously from their experience and their considerable support.

If you have time; money; an accessible, easy market for your books; and/or managing and marketing know-how, self-publishing may be the route for you.

The how-to of self publishing is beyond the scope of this book. The Author-Publisher Network, an information network for self-publishers, will be able to give you the information you need. Have fun, and good luck.

If you want to sell to a publisher, stay with me.

SMALL PRESSES

There is a third viable alternative that falls somewhere between publishing with a mainstream publishing house and self-publishing, and that is to publish with a small press.

Small presses, including regional, specialist and university presses, are often located outside the big cities. The reputable small publishers are listed in *The Writers' and Artists' Yearbook* and *The Writer's Handbook,* so you can check out their credentials. Publishing with a small press combines some of the advantages and disadvantages of the other two plans. Let's look at some of them.

It is usually easier to approach small presses without an agent, so that one large step in your process is eliminated. Many small presses are highly specialised so that it is immediately obvious which ones are best suited for your book. For example, they may publish only literary fiction, or poetry, or only religious books, or only books about farming. Their expertise may mean that they will help you make your book as focused and proficient as it possibly can be for the market you want to reach.

Small presses do, however, have less money (and, obviously, fewer staff) than the major publishers. They may not be able to pay you an advance against royalties. Since they do not have large sales teams, their distribution may not be as widespread or as efficient as that of larger publishers, and they usually lack the financial ability to give you much assistance with your marketing and promotion. However, they do take care of all the design and production details for which you have neither time nor money. Sometimes they allow you to become more involved with the title choice and jacket design, and they tend to be flexible and open to ideas and innovation. Also, you are likely to have closer personal contact with the staff than is often the case with larger publishers, and this can be very rewarding.

A small press might be an excellent alternative for you if you want to be reasonably entrepreneurial with the marketing of your book but lack the financial resources or the interest to edit, design and print it; if you know that your book has a specialised audience that fits into the focus of a particular press; or if you have tried un-successfully to place your book with a major publisher but find that small presses are more receptive.

Small presses are springing up in profusion these days, largely because of changes in the publishing industry over the past few years (though it's worth remembering that some small presses appear almost overnight and vanish without trace – there are no guarantees in publishing). Major houses are less likely to take risks than they once were and are concentrating most of their efforts, especially in fiction, on books they believe will have wide commercial appeal. That leaves out many wonderful books, and small presses are taking up the slack. They publish many thousands of worthwhile books and can give you all the satisfaction of being published without some of the pressures often involved when you work with larger publishers. And if your book sells well with a small press, they may even be able to sell reprint rights to a big commercial house.

Increasingly, small press publishing is viewed as a sound and even prestigious alternative to large, commercial publishers.

BEWARE VANITY

So what if self-publishing isn't an option for you, and you haven't been able to find either an agent to represent you or a mainstream publisher for your book? In those circumstances, advertisements purporting to be from publishing houses desperate to offer you a contract can look very tempting. It's certainly always flattering to believe that someone thinks your book is worth publishing. But be warned. Vanity publishers are in business to make money – but for themselves, not for you.

Vanity publishers work in the following way: An author sends in a manuscript and receives in return an extremely glowing editorial report and/or a letter promising to publish the book – for a fee of on average up to £8,000. This fee is supposed to be a subsidy towards the cost of the book's production and, typically, will be payable 30 per cent up front and 30 per cent on receipt of the proofs of the book, with the remainder upon publication. For unagented authors desperate to find a publisher, this may seem an offer too good to turn down, especially when the royalties on offer are 10 or even 20 per cent higher than those offered by mainstream publishers. However, it is simply not in the interests of vanity publishers to sell or promote your book. It is not unknown for vanity-published books to sell not a single copy. Selling and promotion cost time, effort and money, which vanity publishers are not prepared to provide. Once they have your money, as far as they are concerned their part of the bargain is fulfilled.

Vanity publishers will publish anything, regardless of its quality. They will not provide you with editorial support or advice to make your book better and therefore more saleable; they know that their product will never reach the marketplace, so there would be little point. They will send you several handsome bound 'author copies' of your book when it is eventually published – but these may be virtually the only copies of your book that ever see the light of day. It is common vanity publishing practice for printed sheets to lie unbound and unsaleable in a warehouse. Contractually vanity publishers may be obliged only to print your book, not to bind it. Books won't be bound until the publishers receive cash orders for a specific quantity – which may be never. And don't forget, these are books that you, the author, have personally paid to have produced. The publisher may also undertake to send out review copies; again, this is a meaningless promise, as vanity-published books are never,

ever reviewed. Vanity publishers rarely invest in distribution or marketing, so your book is unlikely to make it into the bookshops (all of which are extremely sceptical about stocking vanity-published books in any case). If you are to sell any copies of your book, you will have to do it without the help of your publisher.

If your book has any real commercial potential, it will find a legitimate publisher – or, if you are prepared to make the commitment, you can self-publish and control the whole project yourself. Vanity publishing exists purely to appeal to your vanity. It is only for those who absolutely have to see their book in print, no matter what the cost.

The Professional Authors' and Publishers' Association was specifically set up to protect self-publishing authors against unscrupulous vanity/subsidy publishers. The Association provides a 'respectable' imprint together with professional production, promotion and marketing services. It might be worth considering this option.

STEP 6 (OR 12)

Write Your Book

Time required: Six months to six years.

For non-fiction writers, the order of the steps I am suggesting here is optional. You may be writing your manuscript now or at Step 12, after you have sold a proposal. Fiction writers, however, should work through these steps in order.

WHEN TO WRITE YOUR BOOK

First-time *fiction* writers will virtually always have to complete a manuscript before attempting to sell it. However, if you are writing non-fiction, you have two options: (1) You may choose to write all or part of your book before you attempt to sell it to a publisher, or, (2) you may begin by writing a proposal for your book, then sell the project to a publisher and receive a royalty advance, and only then write the book, thereby being paid, in effect, to write the book.

The advantage of writing all or a substantial part of your book first is that it will make your proposal far easier to write and possibly also stronger and more effective. Since a book grows and changes as you write it, if you complete your project first, your proposal will be a more accurate reflection of your actual book. Also, you must include sample chapters in your proposal anyway. If you have your completed manuscript in front of you, you may select the best written, most distinctive or most compelling portions of the book for your sample, though bear in mind that some publishers prefer to see the first few consecutive chapters. Check with them first.

Another possible advantage of writing your book first is that, if you are not already a seasoned writer, your writing will usually improve as you do more of it, so your proposal will actually be better written than if you make the proposal the first formal piece you write.

If you complete your project before you try to sell it, you will have a much more thorough knowledge of your material, your conviction about the importance of it may be greater, and you will be a more

31

experienced writer when you go to write the proposal. All of these factors might combine to earn you a higher initial royalty advance.

The disadvantage of completing your manuscript before you sell it is that you may end up having to revamp or even totally rewrite the book based on your editor's input. Your editor may feel the book would be improved with a different structure, a different scope, or even a different audience. The publishers may feel that you need more anecdotes or that some chapters could be eliminated.

On the other hand, if you are starting out with a deep knowledge of your material because you have been teaching it or using it every day in your work; you are fairly certain of the best way to organise your information; and you have some evidence that your writing skills are already good; you may be ready to write a proposal for your book, sell it, and only then begin to write it.

The advantages of this second plan are that it adds excitement to the whole project early on; you receive money for your work sooner; and you will be highly motivated to complete the project because you will now have a contract with a due date.

HOW TO WRITE YOUR BOOK: THE BASICS

The most important advice I or anyone can give you about how to write is to start writing. Writing itself is its own best teacher. You can never learn to write by thinking about writing; you have to *write*.

The world of how-to-write books, writing courses, writers groups and writers conferences is huge. If you want to learn how to write, to find your writer's voice or to hone your writing skills, consult other books and teachers, some of which I have listed in the Resources section. Since my aim is to tell you how to get your book published after you have learned how to write it, I will limit my comments here to a few techniques I have found to be especially helpful to myself and my clients.

START NOW TO GATHER AND ORGANISE MATERIAL

Don't wait to start a simple file for gathering ideas and examples. Use either a database on your computer or good old manila folders.

First, sit down and brainstorm topics and sub-topics related to your book. For this book, for example, I was able to list the following topics quite easily in just five minutes:

Agents
Proposals
The sale
Contracts
The publishing industry
Royalties
Book production
Promotion
How to write
Self-publishing

If you are writing fiction, your files may have to do with aspects of the setting or theme of your book. Are you researching the world of art auctions or the Underground or the scrap metal industry? Do you need specific information about the setting of your novel, say Chicago or Rome?

Create a file for each topic.

Now, whenever you read an article or just a paragraph, or you witness a great example of your point in real life, or an idea pops into your head that you quickly jot down, you will have a place to put it! Then, when you get ready to write about that topic, presto! You have sub-topics, ideas and examples all ready for you to start writing.

These topics need not correspond to what will finally end up being chapters in your book. When you get to the point of organising chapters, these topics will help you, but you will probably separate and combine them in a variety of ways. In fact, I always have a folder entitled, 'Organisational Schemes', in which I put ideas for different ways to organise the book.

In gathering information for my relationship books, I had many more file folders than chapters. If an idea didn't fit into an existing folder, I created a new one. I found that when I was gathering data, I wanted my ideas to expand. Only when I came to the stage of organising the way I would present them did I consolidate them. I had file names as broad as 'Marriage and Career' and as narrow as 'Importance of Compliments'.

Always carry paper and pen with you. If you don't capture an idea the moment you get it, you may very well lose it. When I'm at a formal event, I'm certain to have a few index cards and a small pen in my tiny formal handbag next to my lipstick. If I'm on a hike, you'll find a pen and paper in my pocket. At the beach, I bring a towel and my little notebook. A good supply of notepaper is in my car, next to my bed, and always in my bag. Men virtually always have pockets available for this necessity.

When you are working on a book, people will ask you about it. Get them to give you their ideas or experiences related to your topic. Casual conversations have given me many an idea that later ended up in my book, but only because I wrote them down at the time.

Write down enough about the idea so that, when you read it several months hence, you will be able to call the whole idea to mind. Before I learned this, I would come to notes like, 'Maggie's story about the rug. Excellent example!!!!,' but I couldn't recall the story to save my life. Sometimes, I couldn't even figure out who Maggie was!

I like manila folders. They accept newspaper articles, magazine pages, little scraps of paper, faxed memos and copies of e-mail. I don't have to transfer an idea when I file it. Then, when I get to the delicious day when I get into the file to see all the wisdom I have accumulated there, I just sort all the notes into sub-topics and organise the ideas on either a big writing pad or the outlining function of my word processing programme. I paperclip related magazine articles and scraps of paper together and make reference to the bundle on my outline, so that when I am writing my actual text, I am still working from the original scrap of paper or article.

Ideas from books fit into this system quite well, too. As I read, I jot down notes on paper or index cards. On each card, I write the idea, the appropriate file folder (so it will be easy to file when I finish reading that day), and the full book reference (title, author, publisher and page number – I use codes, of course, for quicker jotting). Later, when I come to a card in a file folder, I can flip right to that page and read the full reference.

My friend, Shelley Nelson, is much more hi-tech about her research methods. She has created a database with fields for the topic of her quotation or idea, the book (or other source) from which it comes, the author, the chapter, the quotation or idea itself and comments. The chapter field is a 'drop menu' listing all the available chapters so that she can simply select one rather than having to retype the chapter title every time, and the quotation field scrolls so she can type as much as she needs to. This database is linked to another one that gives complete bibliographic information about each book.

Whatever system you use, the point is, start a simple system right now. If you are going to write a book, you need a way to store ideas that will make them easy to access and organise later on.

HOW TO START WRITING A BOOK

Writing a book seems like such a huge project; the very idea stops some writers. Of course, breaking the project into small steps makes sense, but, 'What small steps?', I've been asked many times.

Here are some suggestions for exactly what to do with the very first few hours you sit down to 'work on your book'. These are steps you can take this week. You don't have to wait until you clear your diary, clean out the garage, organise your files or until all your children have left home. As writer and writing mentor Og Mandino said, 'There is never a good time to start writing your first book. Stop waiting for it.'

In your very first hours, work on Steps 2, 3 and 4. Establish a goal for your book and begin to work on your book's core identity and title.

Next, if you are writing non-fiction, try creating a table of contents. If that seems too formidable, simply list topics you want to cover – big and little. Then see if they fall into any logical pattern or sequence.

Deliberately try several different organisational schemes. For example, present your information chronologically: Here is what you have to know or do first. Next, this. And so on. Then set that aside and try a completely different scheme, say, 'Ten Ways to . . .' or 'Eight Points about . . .' Maybe your topic breaks down into 'aspects', or there is a principle the reader must understand first. Your topic may present an organisational scheme all of its own. The point is, don't go with the first one that occurs to you. Intentionally play around with the organisation as a way to stimulate your creativity. (For more on a variety of organisational schemes, see Step 7.)

If your work is fiction, decide whether you want to begin by playing around with your plot or your characters. Then try one or more of these ideas:

Sketch out your plot, either in outline form, or in prose.

Write the most explosive, dramatic scene you can imagine. Start with the high point, then see what spins out from there. Perhaps this is your beginning.

Write any scene that comes to mind. Write any dialogue you hear. See what this leads to. It might be other scenes, new characters, or more dialogue.

Write freely and spontaneously for ten minutes. Then see what images, words, or snippets leap out at you when you read what you have written. Work with these charged particles. Write more about them.

Be careful not to be overly logical in the early stages. This is a time to play, to imagine, to open up your material. Later you'll bring in your logical mind to decide you don't need a scene or a character, but not yet. Don't close off any avenue of exploration too soon. Write about what excites you.

For each character, write a complete 'backstory'. Sketch out the life story of the character. Let's say it's a man. Where and how did he grow up? What kind of childhood did he have? Describe his main relatives and friends, his personality characteristics, his work life, his relationship history. Some of this information may never come into play in your novel, but you need to become intimately acquainted with each of your characters so their behaviour in your novel will be consistent with who you know them to be.

The next few times you sit down to work on your book, either repeat the above steps and keep experimenting with them, or take one of the topics you feel very interested in and write a little chapter on it. No censoring or editing yet. Just write.

Now, you've started! You can actually tell your friends you are writing a book!

The significant principle at work in getting started on your book – and in staying with it – is this: Inspiration comes while you are *working* – NOT while you are thinking about working. You have to immerse yourself in your material to get insights, to bring clarity out of chaos or vagueness, and to stimulate your excitement and motivation. So start! If you truly have the passion you need to complete a book, the momentum you set in motion will keep you going.

FOLLOW THE BASIC O-W-E OF WRITING

The basic building blocks of writing, for both fiction and non-fiction, are Outline-Write-Edit, and like the blocks in a building, they must be used in that order. Don't try to put the roof on before you build the walls.

If you are doing stream-of-consciousness writing, you won't use an outline. But if you want to convey a story or concept to anyone else, organise it first.

Don't be intimidated by the word 'outline'. It doesn't have to be that formal thing you learned at school with all the Roman numerals and upper and lowercase letters in the right place. Sometimes my outline is a single page with little pieces of paper stuck all over it with Sellotape. Most word processing programmes have an outline function that makes outlining really easy and facilitates the transition from outline to text.

However you do it, you have to outline. At least 50 per cent of good writing, whether fiction or non-fiction, is good organisation. Often, organising what you are going to say is the hugest part of the challenge. Once you work out the plan, the writing flows easily. Outlining prevents you from writing twenty pages on a very small topic that suddenly fascinates you and only one page on something much more significant.

Of course, your organisation will probably change as you write. When you get into an idea, you may realise you needed to explain it earlier in the chapter, or that it fits far better in another chapter altogether. Still, create your blueprint to the best of your ability before you start.

Then write, uncritically and non-judgmentally. Get your concepts down on paper. The most common mistake beginning writers make is trying to edit to perfection as they are writing. Editing as you go is a mistake because it interrupts your flow of thought, it slows you down, it may take the fun out of writing, and most of all, you can't edit appropriately until you have your whole piece completed. Dianna Booher, who is a prolific writer, suggests that you not even allow yourself to read what you have just written. Keep moving forward, she says. I follow her rule sometimes, and find it is a good discipline for getting a lot of pages written in a day. However, often when I'm stuck, if I go back and read right up to the stuck place, the next words flow logically.

In any case, when you are writing, keep writing. If you need to stop to organise some more, that's fine. But I find that if I've been staring at my computer screen for ten minutes, or making false starts on a paragraph a dozen times because I just can't quite get it right, the only way for me to move through those stuck places is to keep writing. Eventually, either the right words come, or I can get through that spot with a low-quality paragraph, move on to the next material that I *can* write, and then return later to the part that wasn't working.

Don't let yourself get caught up in editing or in perfection while you are writing. Both your writing and your editing will be more successful and more pleasurable if you separate the two tasks.

Editing and rewriting is the third stage of writing. Sometimes you will rewrite many times. Sometimes, the first thing you wrote is brilliant and can't be improved upon.

DON'T START AT THE BEGINNING

Many writers find it easier to begin writing somewhere in the middle of their outline. Try starting with chapter two, or with some chapter later on that you are eager to write. Chapter 1 will end up being both more appropriate and easier to write if you wait until you have some of the other portions of your book complete before writing it.

USE AN EDITOR OR WRITING CONSULTANT

Unless you are a seasoned, published writer, you will benefit greatly by working with an editor or writing consultant.

Writing is a two-person job. Even if you are a skilled editor of your own work, a second skilled editor will make suggestions you will inevitably miss, simply because, as the author, you lose a certain amount of objectivity.

After you sell your project, you will be able to work with the professional editor assigned to you by your publishing house, usually the editor who acquired your book for the house. However, your work must already be in superb condition before you sell it if you hope to be successful.

An editor or writing consultant will teach you a great deal as the two of you bring your work up to professional quality. Even though you may have confidence in your own writing, you don't know what you aren't seeing. A professional partner can be a valuable aide.

If you are a fiction writer and hope to sell your work, working with a qualified, experienced coach is critically important. Choose a coach who knows not only how to write good fiction but also what the current market for fiction is like. If your book can be adapted so that it fits into a genre that has an established market, such as romance, mystery, science fiction, legal thrillers, techno-thrillers or fantasy, your chances of selling your work may be greatly enhanced. Let a professional guide you as you write. I discuss writing and selling fiction more thoroughly at the end of Step 7.

The Writers' and Artists' Yearbook and *The Writer's Handbook* list many editors and editorial services. I will say more about how to contact editors and writing consultants and how to work with them in Step 9 about finding a literary agent.

FREE YOURSELF FROM INTERRUPTIONS WHEN YOU WRITE

If you are the mother of two toddlers and you write at your kitchen table, I can see you laughing out loud at this suggestion. Okay, it isn't always possible. But I've worked with writers who *could* work uninterrupted and have trouble choosing to do so. In the age of answer phones and voice mail, there is no reason that any random caller should have priority over your precious writing time. Don't answer the phone! I put a message on my voice mail that tells my callers I am on a writing schedule and can't talk on the phone during the days, and that I return calls in the late afternoon. I find it is universally respected.

And don't forget about notes on the door. 'Writing time. Please do not disturb except in dire emergency.' They work in both home and office.

Once you can discipline yourself to avoid intruders while you write, you'll love it. And so will your muse.

WAYS TO SKIP THIS STEP ALTOGETHER AND NEVER WRITE A WORD

If you have a story to tell or information to give to the public, but you are not a writer and you haven't the time or interest to become one, there definitely are ways to 'write' a book without having to write it.

One alternative is to organise your material and then speak one section or one chapter at a time into a tape recorder. Have it transcribed, and then edit yourself, or hire a professional writer or editor to polish it up for you.

Another option is to use a ghostwriter or co-author. Both of these are perfectly respectable, effective alternatives.

How do you find a ghostwriter or co-author?

If you are famous or well-positioned, or what you have to say is of obvious interest to the public, you might try calling or writing a literary agent and presenting your idea. If the agent sees potential in it, he or she may be eager to help you find a collaborator.

If you need to find a collaborator on your own, look in the classified ads of writers' magazines, advertise in appropriate places on the Internet, search through the authors' handbooks in your local library, look in the acknowledgment section of books in your field, or contact a journalist who has written about your work.

Writing collaborations can be wonderful for both parties, but they can also be difficult. Be sure you have an excellent collaboration agreement (the Society of Authors will be able to help you with this) before you begin to work.

*   *   *

You'll find more about how to avoid the pitfalls and reap the joys of writing in Part II. And all those great books in the How to Write section of the bookshop will inspire you too. But in the end, it all boils down to one word: Write. Immerse yourself in your work. To that I would only add, surround yourself with positive, encouraging people, and share early versions of your work only with people whose opinion you have reason to respect.

Write, write, write!

Write a Book Proposal

Time required: From one month to one year.
(From the day you actually begin to write it.)

A book proposal is a sales tool. It needs to be outstanding because there is enormous competition for your book in the marketplace. Your proposal must convince agents and editors that your book soars above the pack.

If you have not already written your book, the proposal-writing process will also help you to focus and organise your ideas, become familiar with your competition, and test-market your ideas, so that when you begin writing the book, much of the difficult work will have been completed.

The proposal outline I present here is effective for non-fiction books. (For fiction, see the section at the end of Step 7.) If you have an excellent book idea and you follow this outline closely, you are likely to have good results. Feel free to deviate from this outline if you find that changes or additions are necessary or they add character and originality to your proposal.

To be successful, a proposal must

- present an idea that has commercial potential, that is, it has a wide enough potential audience to sell a substantial number of books.
- be tightly written. It must offer a lot of information in a way that is highly accessible and efficient.
- be well-organised and demonstrate obvious internal logic.
- reflect the tone and writing style of the final book.
- convey enthusiasm and excitement.

The following outline will help you to accomplish all these goals.

I shall present the parts of the proposal in the order in which they will appear in the final presentation. Obviously, you will work on it in a different order. It is wise to work on the competitive books section early so that you have a good idea whether any book already in the marketplace comes close to yours. Sometimes, it can be very encouraging to read other books on your topic because you realise you do have an original or better approach. Also, reading other books on your topic will stimulate your own creativity.

On the other hand, more than once I've received phone calls from authors in great distress, saying, 'Oh no! I feel awful! I found a book exactly like the one I want to write.'

Usually such a discovery is not fatal for your book idea. When you actually read the book, you will find that the subject has been treated very differently from the way you will treat it. Besides, that book is on the shelves now; your book is a year or more away from publication. Regard other books like yours as a challenge to find a distinctive, original approach.

I suffered 'my book's been written' heartbreak quite a few times during the six years I was writing *If I'm So Wonderful, Why Am I Still Single?* How to find a partner is, as editors love to say, a 'crowded market'. But does that mean that there will never again be a book written for singles who would like to be coupled? I seriously doubt it. Somehow, there is always room for one more book – if it is distinctive, exciting, and stands apart.

Another part of the proposal you will want to address early is your table of contents and chapter-by-chapter outline. As you work, you may revise these over and over, but remember, inspiration comes while you are working. You won't see how you can improve upon an organisational scheme or a flow of ideas until you begin to work with it. So start working. The book will take shape, and new ideas are bound to emerge.

THE NON-FICTION PROPOSAL

1. TITLE PAGE

Centre your title and subtitle nice and big. Under that write, 'A Book Proposal by (your name)'. Towards the bottom of the page, put your name, address, all possible phone numbers, and your fax number and e-mail address if appropriate. Make yourself very easy to reach. Editors and agents are busy. If they have to search for your access data (in a cover letter that became separated from the proposal, for example), they may give up. (PS Be sure you have a reliable answering machine or voice mail service with an efficient, professional message at the other end of your phone number. Busy signals and no answers are deadly in this business.)

Some imaginative graphics on your title page are okay, but don't get carried away. Unless your book is about something very wild or funny or beautiful that you want to convey with the title page, stay businesslike. It's far more critical to convey your originality with strong words inside than with a memorable title page – and forgettable copy.

2. CONTENTS OF THE PROPOSAL

The proposal contents page may look something like this (this also gives you an overview of the entire proposal we are about to discuss):

Proposal Contents

Overview	3
The Author	6
The Audience for the Book	7
The Marketing Plan	8
Analysis of the Competition	10
Book's Table of Contents	12
Chapter-by-Chapter Outline	14
Sample Chapters	21

(The sample chapters may be numbered separately, in which case, leave a space and write 'Sample Chapters' with no page number.)

The proposal table of contents immediately shows your readers that you have included all the essential information. Also, it provides them with a map of what they are about to read.

3. OVERVIEW

I like to refer to this section of the proposal as the 'sell page'. The overview is the reason a proposal is so much stronger a sales vehicle than your manuscript itself, because it gives you the opportunity to say not just what your book is about, but why it is important and how it will benefit readers. It is your chance to sell an agent or editor on the value or even the potential greatness of this book.

Professional salespeople distinguish between 'features' and 'benefits'. A feature is, 'This is a blue, high-quality fountain pen.' A benefit is, 'This pen will make you feel wealthy, secure, successful, sophisticated and happy every time you write.'

Your sell page is your opportunity to demonstrate the benefits of your book. How will your book help readers? Why does the world need this book? The chapter-by-chapter outline will give you plenty of opportunity to discuss the actual features of the book later.

I have used the following sell-page formula myself and with numerous clients with outstanding results, and highly recommend it.

If you have completed the first few steps I suggested in this book, you will have a good head start on the sell page, because Step 3, 'Establish Your Book's Identity', asks several of the same questions.

One more note: Write this section of the proposal in the third person. Do not address your reader (an agent or editor) directly as in 'You will see how . . . ,' and do not refer to yourself as 'I' but rather as 'the author'. Different rules will apply to other sections of the proposal, but here, stick to the third person.

Here is the formula for a brilliant sell page:

A. Why is there a need for your book?
For example, what pain are readers experiencing in their lives? What information do they lack? What predicament exists in society? What vacuum longs to be filled? In what new ways could readers be entertained? What's the problem? Where's the void?

State it as dramatically as you can. Begin your overview with a shocking quote by a famous person, a startling statistic, the statement of a familiar problem, or a short anecdote that illustrates your point.

B. How will your book meet this need, resolve this pain, supply this information, explain this predicament, eliminate this vacuum, provide this entertainment, solve this problem or fill this void?
Don't answer these questions with empty hype. We know you think it's a great book idea. Instead, convince us by offering as much actual content as you can in a short paragraph or two.

C. How is your book different from every other book on this general topic? What is your book's original contribution?

D. Why are you the person who should write this book?
What experiences in your life qualify you? How did you gain your expertise or your special knowledge? This is not the place for a full-length bio; that comes later. Here, talk only about your expertise on the topic of the book.

E. How long will the manuscript be, and when will it be ready?
If your book will have an unusual format or size, here is the place to say so. Do you see it as a small book suitable for gift shops? Are you planning a large coffee-table book? Is there anything else unusual about its format?

If your book will contain photographs, illustrations or a large number of charts or graphs, and you have not already mentioned this above, mention it here.

If you would like your book to be published as a quality paperback rather than a hardcover, mention that and say why. For example, is it a book people will want to carry around with them so it needs to be lightweight? Is the audience for this book people who don't have much money so it needs to be affordable? Are books of this type usually published in paperback?

Most authors prefer to be published in hardcover first because, generally, you are paid more for a hardcover up front, and hardcovers are more likely to be reviewed. But these are not rigid rules. You may have a good reason to prefer that your book be published first as a paperback. If you are a first-time author writing genre fiction, your book might find far more readers if it is published as a mass market paperback.

If you envision your book as a normal format, hardcover non-fiction book, then you need only mention the approximate number of pages you envision. If you expect it to be an average size book, just say it will be approximately 200–250 pages. If you expect the book to be unusually long or unusually short, estimate the number of pages as best you can. Readers understand you are estimating; they just need a general idea whether this will be an unusually short or long book.

Finally, tell your reader the status of the manuscript now, if any, and the approximate date you will be able to deliver a completed manuscript.

Often, this entire 'specifications' paragraph will be one or two sentences long, something like, 'A first draft of the manuscript is complete (or one-third complete, or whatever; if you haven't begun to write, omit this). The finished book will be approximately 250 pages. The author will be able to deliver the manuscript by *(date)*,' or 'by one year from the sale of the project.'

F. Close

Don't end your fabulous sell page with this dry information about page count and delivery date. Add a short closing paragraph or sentence that sums up the benefits of this book – without being repetitive – and reminds your reader of its importance.

You can write an excellent overview or 'sell page' in two to six double-spaced pages. Rarely will you need more than this. If your overview is longer, review it to see whether you have repeated yourself, told too long a story, given superfluous details, or offered too many examples. Remember, agents and editors have hundreds of proposals to read. Your aim is to excite them about your project in as few words as possible.

4. THE AUTHOR

For non-fiction writers, the days when you can just write an excellent book are gone. Nowadays, you have to be an expert.

You have to be an expert because you will be competing against other books written by experts. Why should the public read yours?

You have to be an expert because you are much easier to promote if you have worked with children for forty years, or you just walked across Africa, or you made a million pounds, or have taught more than ten thousand people how to swim, or you teach at a university.

So what if you aren't an expert?

Become one. You can probably enhance your credentials without too much additional effort beyond what you will need to do to write your book anyway. Begin right now to conduct workshops and to interview experts on your book topic.

In addition to establishing your credibility, both these activities are superb ways to gather anecdotes and to test and expand your ideas. They will greatly enrich your writing. After a year's worth of workshops and fifty interviews, you will actually be much more of an expert, and you can sound like one by describing the workshops and interviews in your author bio.

Write articles, and get them published in the magazines or journals relevant to your topic. Join organisations that will expand your knowledge and look good in your author credentials. Conduct a study using questionnaires, interviews or actual experiments.

If you still feel your credentials are weak, or you don't want to take the time to expand them, other options are available. For example, you can collaborate with someone who is an expert, even if you still do most of the work. Or you might recruit someone who is an expert to write a foreword for your book (see Step 8). This will increase your credibility with agents and editors and your marketability with the public.

However, if you care enough about a topic to write a book on it, you probably are an expert already! All you need to do is convey this in the author section of your proposal.

Have you been through a life experience that taught you valuable lessons you now want to share?

Have you interviewed (or do you plan to interview) many people and to organise and relate what you learned from these interviews?

In the author section of the proposal, emphasise your topic expertise, your writing experience, if any, and your speaking, teaching or media background, if any. But also give the reader a fuller picture of who you are. Don't include a boring résumé. Instead, in a chatty and compelling style, reveal your most important achievements and the most interesting aspects of your background.

Again, it is usually most effective to write this section in the third person, speaking about 'the author'. It is easy to sound too self-serving if you have to keep saying, 'I did this and I won that.' However, I have seen author sections written in the first person that were effective. You can become more personal and intimate with your reader, and can make statements like, 'I know this works because . . .' or 'I am most effective in situations when I . . .' If you do it well, you can come across as confident rather than self-aggrandising. Third person is the standard, but feel free to experiment and see which feels better to you.

5. THE AUDIENCE FOR THE BOOK

This section might also be called, 'The Market for the Book'. In other words, who will be interested in reading it? What evidence can you offer that people will buy it?

Conduct some simple research and use numbers.

How many people belong to organisations or subscribe to magazines about your topic? What books related to your subject sold very well, thereby demonstrating the public's thirst for books on this topic? If you can demonstrate that your subject is especially timely, do so. Did a cover story about it recently appear in a popular magazine? From census data, how many people in the general population are potential readers? (New mothers, singles, farmers, entrepreneurs, theatregoers, artists, etc.)

If your book will appeal to a variety of groups, give us statistics about each of those groups. For example, in a proposal for a book about getting new clients by referrals from current clients, the author said the book would be helpful to insurance brokers, estate agents, solicitors, stockbrokers, etc. He listed twelve such groups. Then he told us how many practitioners there were in each of these groups. The total turned out to be a sizeable chunk of the population who could benefit from the information in the book and to whom the book could be specifically marketed.

In the age of the Internet, you may be able to find your answers online. But don't forget about reference librarians. They can be extremely helpful, either in finding statistics for you or in directing you to sources. Private polling organisations and trade associations within a particular industry may also be able to help you.

Be highly factual and realistic in this section. Truly do your homework, and make it obvious that you mean business. This is not the place for hyperbole, meaningless generalisations or sloppy assertions.

When you write up this section, organise and format your information so it is easy to read at a glance. Use lists with bullet points, boldface type for subheadings, short paragraphs, and even simple graphs or graphics if they are genuinely helpful.

6. MARKETING AND PROMOTION

In many proposals, your ideas about marketing your book will not be a separate section but will be included in the 'audience' section above.

Identifying the market for the book implies that it should be promoted to those specific groups.

However, if you know something about promoting books and have some ingenious, novel ideas; you already work with a publicist; you have an unusual ability to sell many copies of your own book, or, most important, you are planning to commit a substantial amount of your own money to the promotion of this book, you can dazzle an editor by demonstrating your savvy, your commitment, and your willingness to work.

An impressive marketing plan, professionally and convincingly presented, will sell virtually any book. If the publisher sees that you are capable of and committed to marketing your own books in substantial numbers, why wouldn't they take a risk on you?

For example, do you belong to an organisation that might be appropriate for a direct mailing? Can you think of organisations with newsletters in which you might advertise or write an article? Do you speak frequently to large groups of people to whom you can sell your book at the 'back of the room'? Could you sell books in bulk to organisations that might use them for gifts, awards or even required reading? Are you addressing an industry that has lots of conventions where you might speak or have a stand to sell books? Do you produce a newsletter in which you could make a special offer to your readers? Do you regularly offer workshops so that you have a 'following' of people who will want to buy your book? Do you have your own mailing list?

If you have a connection with any well-known experts in your field who might endorse your book, list those people and your connection with them in this section.

If you plan to conduct special marketing or promotion of your book yourself, by all means lay out your plan in detail here. If not, feel free to omit this section or to put a paragraph about your promotional ideas in the section on 'The Audience'.

7. ANALYSIS OF THE COMPETITION

Agents and editors are well-read, but they cannot be intimately familiar with every subject on earth. You need to help them evaluate the marketability of your book by telling them exactly what the competition for your book is. At the same time, of course, you will explain how your book sets itself apart from all the others.

List specific books including the publisher, publication year, current cover price and format (hardcover or paperback). After each title, describe it in two or three sentences, mention its strengths and shortcomings with the emphasis on the latter, and then explain exactly how your book is different and/or better.

Three to eight books is usually sufficient, listed in the order of their importance. Most of them should be recent, published within the last three or four years. Include an older book if it is still widely available and well-known, especially if is something of a classic in its field.

In the sample proposal I have included in Part III, you will see how to format your competitive books section. You may decide it is sufficient to comment on each individual book. Or you may wish to open this section with a paragraph in which you summarise the distinctive features of your book and then comment on each book in addition.

In your comments about each book, be sure to make a statement about your own book every time. Don't simply describe the other book and assume your reader will see what the differences are. Sometimes it is hard to avoid being repetitive in these statements about your own book, but work on using them to your best advantage. Every competitive book gives you an opportunity to make a new compelling point about your own book. Don't waste it.

How do you find these books? You will already know many of them because of your general interest in your field. But be sure you conduct research too, so that some recent book doesn't slip by you. Browse thoroughly in several large bookshops. Look through your topic in *Books in Print* (available at your library).

You must also list any significant books on your topic that are about to be published. To research these, look in *The Bookseller* (the trade magazine of the publishing industry, which can be ordered through your local newsagents).

In general, it is a good idea to become friendly with an independent bookseller in your area. Generally speaking, large chain bookshops are managed by business people, not literary types. Independent bookshop owners are in this business because they love books. They select the books they want to stock, and they have a deep knowledge of the whole book world. A friendly independent bookseller can be helpful to you in many different stages of your book writing and publishing process, offering you, for example, an educated opinion on everything from your subject matter and title ideas to your jacket design and your promotional plans.

If you have established a relationship with a bookseller, ask him or her whether you might browse through current catalogues from several of the major publishing houses. Every publishing house provides all bookshops with a catalogue of titles they will publish in the next six months or so. It is from these catalogues that booksellers order the books they want to stock. You will find it generally enlightening to browse through recent catalogues, and you will be able to spot any forthcoming titles that might be competition for yours.

Never omit a book because it is too similar to yours and you hope the agents and editors won't know about it. Agents and editors know everything, and you will damage your credibility if you try to slip one past them. If a book is very close to yours in subject matter, use it to demonstrate the popularity of the topic, and then find *something* distinctive about your own book. Have you organised it differently? Is yours funnier or more accessible? Does the other book omit something important that you include? Are your credentials on this topic better than the other author's? Is your core message or your whole approach different? Is your book more timely or more comprehensive?

In the unlikely situation that you honestly can't come up with anything singular about your book, consider this a gift from the gods. Return to the drawing board and work with your idea until you do come up with a unique angle. You will almost certainly be inspired in ways that will vastly improve your book.

You may be excited if you encounter the other extreme: no competition whatsoever for your book. But remember: editors, who are looking for reasons to reject books, could interpret this as meaning there is no market for your book. Just be sure you demonstrate convincingly, in your 'audience' section and again here, that there is a huge need for your book and that you are the brilliant person who arrived on the scene first.

8. RESOURCES REQUIRED

For most books, this section of the proposal is inappropriate and should be skipped.

However, if, in order to write your book, you will need to travel extensively or conduct expensive research, and you are proposing that the publisher help finance the travel or research, outline your plans and their exact cost in this separate section. In fact, publishers rarely pay separately for research or travel, but they might take it into consideration when establishing your royalty advance. Especially in the case of major biographies, publishers often take research expenses into account.

9. BOOK'S TABLE OF CONTENTS

Now you come to the 'features' portion of your book proposal. Exactly how will the book be organised and what will it say?

The simple table of contents, on one page if possible, accomplishes several tasks. It allows your reader to see your book's content and organisation at a glance. Also, it may contain indications of your general style. For example, you may have amusing or clever or literary chapter titles that will entice the reader.

At least 50 per cent of the genius of a good non-fiction book is its organisation. Put another way, at least 50 per cent of the job of writing a good non-fiction book is organising it well. You may have a wonderful idea. But if you present it in a way that doesn't follow easily from one idea to the next or that has no easily discernible internal logic, or, perhaps most offensive, that is highly repetitive, you will lose readers. Agents and editors know this. They are looking for books with logical, well-communicated and fresh organisation. It isn't enough for you to see the organisational logic of your book yourself; you must be able to make your organisational plan obvious and easily accessible to your readers.

In Step 6 where I suggested ways to get started on your book project, I made a recommendation I will remind you of here, for it is a tool many of my clients have found to be extremely useful.

Try out a variety of organisational schemes. To do so will stimulate your creativity. Work hard on one organisational plan, finding the appropriate place for every major idea. Then, set that aside and try an entirely different scheme. When you find that an element fits into three or four different spots equally well, see if that problem suggests a variation on your scheme.

Even if you eventually return to your original plan, you will generate ideas by experimenting.

For example, I have a friend who after interviewing more than thirty women who had never married, wrote a book about women who make this choice. At first she thought she would organise her book according to the issues these women face: family pressures, socialising in a couples-oriented society, children in their lives, etc. But she found it clumsy to keep flipping around from one woman's story to another and to manage so many interviews for each topic.

Next, she tried telling each woman's individual story in more detail. She found this became repetitive. Another idea she tried was a two-part book: what women like about not marrying, and what they don't like. At one point, she thought she would make it more prescriptive, and she tried Ten Lessons from Women Who Have Never Married. This she found to be too limiting; she was left with important parts of the story that didn't fit anywhere.

What worked best for her in the end was dividing her subject matter into age groups: A World of Possibilities: Women in Their Twenties; Life Directions: Women in Their Thirties; Surprise, Panic, and Joy: Women in Their Forties; Relaxing and Letting Go: Women in Their Fifties. And so on.

For most subjects, a large number of organisational plans might work. Keep trying different ones until you feel certain you have the best one.

Even after you settle on your favourite organisational scheme, be assured that as you write your book, it will change. No one will ever hold you to the exact chapter outline you present in your proposal. You will find yourself changing the order of chapters, eliminating some and adding others as you write.

However, in the table of contents you present in your proposal, you must make your organisational scheme obvious and easy to follow. You may find it helpful to divide your book into several parts or sections, each with its own title.

Create chapter titles that are explanatory. If you want to be clever too, try using a subtitle. For example, in *If I'm So Wonderful, Why Am I Still Single?*, I wanted to use the idea that 'you have to kiss a lot of frogs' to find your prince or princess. But my 'frog' titles didn't convey enough about what was in the chapter. So I used subtitles:

PART II – GUIDELINES FOR KISSING FROGS

Chapter 5   Don't Get Stuck in the Swamp
Learning to Say No

Chapter 6   Watch for Frogs in Royal Clothing
             *Distinguishing Between Pseudo-Intimacy and the
             Real Thing*

Chapter 7   Beware of the Vanishing Prince or Princess
             Avoiding Commitmentphobes

Chapter 8   Don't Try to Make the Prince or Princess Love
             You
             How to Handle an Intimacy Gap

Chapter 9   What to Do When You Find Your Prince or
             Princess But You Are Afraid of the Castle
             Learning to Say Yes

10. CHAPTER-BY-CHAPTER OUTLINE

Now you will write a page or so, double-spaced, about what you plan to do in each chapter. Offer enough actual content to intrigue your reader and to convey what you will be discussing, but remember also that your ability to be convincing in as few words as possible will be appreciated and rewarded. Publishers are looking for writers who can write tightly, without repetition or rambling. If you truly need more than a page or two, go ahead, but be sure you truly need it.

Summarise your chapter ever so briefly. State your premise and then explain how you will expand upon it. Don't hesitate to use lists, bullet points, or subtitles if they will help to clarify your organisation or make your intentions easily accessible to your reader.

You may want to start each chapter summary in the same way you will start the actual chapter. If anecdotes and examples will be a part of your book, include some in your chapter summaries. If each chapter will begin with a quotation, consider starting your chapter summaries that way.

If excellent organisation of ideas is 50 per cent of a good book, the other 50 per cent is passion about those ideas. Your chapter summaries must show that you are excited about your subject matter, knowledgeable and able to convey your passion in a way that is contagious.

When you've reached this section of the proposal, it's appropriate to write in the second person. If your book will address the reader directly sometimes, feel free to use that form in your chapter summary. It is also appropriate to flip back and forth between addressing the book reader and the proposal reader. For example:

> The period after you have had major surgery is filled with anxieties that are quite different from the ones you had before your surgery. As one patient said, 'I thought the end of the surgery would be the end of the worries. Instead, it turned out to be the beginning of a whole new set of problems.' If you know ahead of time what to anticipate, you can plan accordingly, and you will have a much easier time after surgery.
>
> Chapter seven will discuss the following common but usually unanticipated post-surgical management problems:
>
> - Problem A
>   Solutions to Problem A that will be described
> - Problem B
>   Solutions to Problem B

The chapter summary is mostly about the 'features' of your book, but don't hesitate to sneak in some benefits too, as you describe what you will write. Convey enthusiasm. Always be aware you are selling this idea to a sceptic. Make every word count.

11. SAMPLE CHAPTERS

Ask the agents or editors to whom you are sending your proposal whether they would prefer to see the first few consecutive chapters – so that they can see how you are planning to develop your argument or ideas as the book unfolds – or whether it is okay to send just the chapter or chapters you feel represent your best work. If your chapters are fairly long, and similar to each other in structure, one complete chapter may be enough. However, a single or introductory chapter often doesn't give agents or editors enough of a feel of the 'meat' of the book, which is why they may need to see more material in order to assess your project.

No matter how many chapters you send, be sure that they are extremely well organised and that they keep making their organisational scheme obvious to the reader. And each chapter must convey its own passion. A book needs a balance of emotional content and logic. Be sure your sample chapter or chapters have both.

PREPARING AND MAILING YOUR PROPOSAL

After you have completed Steps 8 and 9 and you are ready to mail out your proposal, here's how to do it.

FORMAT

Your completed proposal should be double-spaced with ample margins so it is very easy to read. Use a header in smaller type in the upper left corner of every page, something like 'John Jones Proposal' or 'The Sex Life of Dinosaurs – Proposal'. Number the pages consecutively, including your sample chapters. It's best not to start again at page one with your sample chapters, but this is acceptable.

Do not bind or fasten your proposal in any way. Buy a large 'manuscript-size' rubber band at your local stationers and put that around it. Or use a large clip. Your proposal will be easier to read if pages can be placed on the bottom as they are read. Also, if you are lucky, your agent will want to copy your proposal so others can review it. She will definitely need to copy it when she sends it out to editors.

ENCLOSURES

You may want to enclose with your proposal a few press clippings about you and your work, proof of awards you have received, testimonial letters from clients, brochures that describe your presentations or services, or other material that offers evidence of your experience and competence. Such enclosures are not at all necessary, but if they are impressive or informative, do include some. Don't flood an agent with these extras, however. Be selective. She will know this isn't all the supplementary material you have.

COVER LETTER

A cover letter is an essential courtesy, but it should be brief. All vital information including your address and phone number must be in the proposal itself.

If you were referred by someone the agent knows, by all means remind her of that. If the agent requested your proposal after receiving a query from you (see Step 9), thank her for her interest.

Set a warm tone. Mention the title and what type of book it is. If you like, use or adapt the two-sentence pitch you have developed to grab your reader's attention right away.

One or two paragraphs is plenty. Entice your reader, but don't use the cover letter to do the job that the proposal itself must do.

SAE

Always include a self-addressed, stamped envelope with your proposal. Most agents receive hundreds of proposals, and sending even standard rejection letters to every writer can become a major expense.

If you want your proposal returned to you should it not be accepted, include a large enough envelope and sufficient postage. However, if you want to send a fresh copy to any new agent, you may not care about having this one returned. In that case, enclose a regular business envelope. If you like, attach a little sticky-note saying, 'Not necessary to return proposal.'

PACKAGING

Put your proposal in a package that is easy to open. A padded envelope with a tear-strip opener is ideal. Use only five staples and no tape to seal the envelope. Don't make your agent work to get into your dazzling sell-page opener.

THE FICTION PROPOSAL

As a first-time fiction author, you will usually want to complete your manuscript before you begin to shop it around. You will still use a query letter to attract the attention of agents at first. (See Step 9.) But when an agent expresses interest in your work, you will want to have a completed manuscript ready, or an excellent first half.

Typically, if your query sparks her interest, an agent will want to see a plot synopsis and the first three chapters of your novel. If she likes that, she will want to see the rest of the book.

TYPES OF FICTION

The three main categories of fiction are literary, mainstream and genre. Literary fiction does not rely heavily on plot for its appeal, but instead on the strength and power of the writing. Characters tend to be complex and filled with nuance. Literary novels are read not so much for action as for superb writing, rich character development and originality of vision.

Mainstream novels appeal to a broad popular audience and do depend more on plot for their appeal. The writing is generally high quality but also very accessible. Characters must be well-developed, not stereotyped.

Genre novels depend almost entirely on plot and less on quality writing or character development. Editors usually want them to stay fairly close to a standard formula that they know readers expect. What matters in genre writing is the suspense of the story line. Some common genres are romance, mystery, science fiction, legal or techno-thrillers, fantasy and supernatural.

Of course some novels don't fit tidily into one of these categories but are actually a blend of several of them – or may carve out new territory altogether. One of the most common reasons agents give for rejecting fiction is that it doesn't fit into a standard genre or category and will therefore be very difficult to sell to the public. This is an exasperating situation that discourages creativity and quashes innovation. Agents and editors say, 'Don't blame us. The public won't buy it.' But of course new ideas have to start somewhere. If no one ever had the courage to try something new, we'd still be reading only epic poems and gothic novels. If your idea and your writing are sensational, don't let the genre problem stop you, but anticipate it. In your query letter, make a strong case for the power, appeal and saleability of your new category or blend of categories.

THE FICTION QUERY LETTER

When you have completed your novel and are ready to look for agents, the tool you will need is not a proposal, but a query letter.

Your fiction query letter should be one single-spaced page, no longer. Your aim is to entice an agent in as concise and businesslike a way as possible.

In the first paragraph of the query letter, give the agent all of the following vital information: title, number of pages, category of fiction, tone or type of writing (historical, satirical, humorous, inspirational, poetic, etc.), and simple plot summary. For example:

> I am seeking representation for a 372-page manuscript entitled *Girlfriends Unite*. This humorous, mainstream novel is the story of three feisty women who are fed up with dating and have decided to take revenge on every man who has ever said, 'I'll call you.'

In the second paragraph, explain why this novel will appeal to a wide audience. If possible, compare your work to highly successful novels with the idea that, if readers liked that one, they will *love* this one. Paragraph two should read like flap copy for your book. In fact, read some published fiction flap copy before you write this paragraph. For example:

> This novel will become a must-read for every woman who has ever dated! Readers will adore this hilarious romp through the ravages and the victories of the singles scene that carefully avoids common man-bashing and takes aim just as much at women as at men. Combining the humour of *First Wives Club* with the wisdom of *Men Are from Mars*, *Girlfriends Unite* captures the deep essence of today's struggle between the sexes.

In paragraph three, offer a brief plot summary. Be sure you actually summarise the plot, not the theme of the book.

> The story begins when Ellen, a 43-year-old divorcée, receives a call from a former boyfriend, Ted. During the course of making her decision about whether to see him, she and her two best friends form a 'consulting firm' for themselves and their confused single women friends. When they realise they can't offer superb service without doing additional research and they begin spying on dates – and then get discovered – the true natures of the men and women involved are clearly revealed. In the end, all three women end up with the men of their dreams – after a manner of speaking.

In paragraph four, talk about yourself, emphasising your expertise with the subject matter in the novel, your writing and publishing background, and any endorsements from established writers you anticipate receiving. If you have unusual ideas for marketing or promoting your book, or any connections that will help you to sell copies, definitely add them.

A college lecturer in English literature for the past twelve years, I spend my college terms commiserating with my single colleagues and my summer vacations writing. My short stories and journalism have appeared in *Cosmopolitan* and *She* magazines. My active involvement in the organisation of the University of Southampton's Annual Writers' Conference will give me the unique opportunity to promote and sell copies of my book.

At the end of the letter, you might want to say, 'I will show my manuscript to only one agent at a time, so if you are interested, please contact me immediately at (phone, fax, e-mail, or address).' (More about this in Step 9.)

THE PLOT SYNOPSIS

If your query letter is successful, agents will usually ask to see a plot summary and the first three chapters of your novel.

The plot synopsis must be just that. Don't discuss the theme of the book, but the actual plot. The mistake most beginners make with plot summaries is becoming too abstract. Let your plot synopsis explain some of the key characters and excite the reader about the story itself. The plot summary should be three to five pages, double-spaced. It must show how the subplots intertwine with the main plot and how all plot lines are resolved.

When you send your plot synopsis and sample chapters, be sure to include a self-addressed envelope with sufficient postage to return everything you sent.

THE REALITIES OF WRITING AND SELLING FICTION

Once your novel is complete, your task of preparing it for presentation to agents is much easier than the corresponding task for non-fiction writers. However, actually making a sale to a publisher is much harder for fiction writers than for non-fiction writers, because there is much more competition and because fiction, being less targeted at a specific market, is more difficult to sell and promote. Fiction is also very subjective and material which receives a prompt rejection by one editor may be highly praised by another.

As a fiction writer, you will do best if you love the process of writing itself, you believe in your work, you have a thick skin and don't let rejections set you back for more than a week or so, and you possess unusual levels of tenacity and patience. One writing consultant I spoke with, who has worked with hundreds of fiction writers for more than fifteen years, told me that most of her published clients were working on their third or fourth novel and had been writing for nine or ten years before they tasted the sweet victory of publication. She emphasised that most novels go through three or four drafts, and that many fiction writers have worked with a creative writing teacher at some point in their writing career.

Of course there are exceptions to every rule, and you could be one of them. But your writing or your subject matter must be extraordinary. Publishers are looking for novels that are extremely well written, have wide commercial appeal and a broad audience.

There is no question it is unfortunate that there isn't a broader readership for creative fiction, and that publishers aren't more interested in taking risks and in working hard to create markets for innovative writing. But until the publishing landscape changes, make the very most of the resources you do have available, and be grateful that you have found a way to express your own deepest passions. You are one of the lucky ones!

Enlist a Famous Person or an Expert to Write a Foreword or Endorsement for Your Book

Time required: At least an hour a week until you succeed.

You may be able to skip this step.

If you already have many years of experience in your subject matter, write a strong 'Author' section in your proposal in which you highlight your strongest achievements and the depth of your experience. Make it crystal clear that *you* are a famous person or an expert and the publisher should feel lucky to be the one who gets to publish your work.

However, if your chief expertise is a personal experience, or you are writing because you have an idea or a story you are burning to share, and if you have never before been published, an endorsement from a respected academic, a well-known author, or a recognised expert in your field on your proposal can really give it an edge over the competition.

Whether or not it is fair or logical, publishers today want credentials. You may be a brilliant writer with breakthrough ideas about, let's say, parenting, because you have just successfully parented two human beings. But if all you can say is that you are a successful parent, chances are you'll end up buried on an editor's or agent's desk with all the other undistinguished proposals.

There are exceptions. If your proposal is stunning enough, you may excite an editor even though you have minimal credentials. But under any circumstances, you will get further faster if you realise that an endorsement from a famous name or an expert on a proposal is like a pound sign to publishers.

Of course, you will want to line up a number of endorsement statements after you complete your book in order to make it more appealing to the public. We will cover that process thoroughly in Step 15. This step is about obtaining an endorsement to make your proposal easier to sell.

So how do you persuade a famous person or an expert to write a foreword for you?

Ask.

If you know anyone who knows anyone who knows anyone, use your connections. But if you don't, ask anyway. Make a list of all the authors, university academics, known experts and celebrities you wish you could persuade, and start thinking of ways to approach them. Use letters and phone calls. Try to meet the person by attending a workshop or lecture. Become friendly with the person's receptionist and see if you can get him or her invested in the success of your endeavour. Tailor your approach to each individual based on what you can learn about his or her beliefs and work. Describe the promotion you are planning for the book, and point out that the endorser will receive good exposure and publicity by becoming a part of your project.

Consider asking a friend who is good at sales and marketing to work out a strategy with you, help you draft letters or even make some phone calls for you.

A strong proposal will help convince prospective endorsers to assist you. Some experts will find your ideas appealing and will feel good about supporting work they respect. Others will realise that endorsing your book will benefit them by giving them additional exposure.

In some cases you may tell your prospect that you will be happy to draft a foreword yourself when the time comes. This makes it easier than ever for the person to support you. Some people will be genuinely interested enough to want to read the manuscript after it is complete and write their own foreword, but it is usually appropriate to offer to draft it yourself.

When you secure a commitment from that special someone to write a foreword for you, ask the person to send you a letter on their formal letterhead simply stating that he or she has agreed to write a foreword for your book. Include this letter with your proposal.

A foreword, by the way, is simply an extended endorsement of you and your book. It states why the book is needed, how expertly the subject matter is handled and why you are well-qualified to write it. It might contain some interesting statistics, a story that illustrates the need for the book, or an anecdote about how the expert knows you. In general, it should make the reader more confident that this book was a good choice, and more eager to read it.

Now, the final, fun step: To the title page of your proposal, under your own name and in large, prominent letters, add the words, 'Foreword by _____   _____'.

Enlist the Services of a Fabulous Literary Agent

Time required: From two to fourteen months after you complete your proposal.

Some well-meaning advisors may tell you that you don't need an agent. Their arguments are some combination of the following:

'You are perfectly capable of approaching publishers yourself. Why in the world would you give away 10 per cent of your money? Agents don't do anything for you that you can't do yourself.

'Besides, the process of finding an agent is far too arduous and time-consuming. You are mostly dependent on networking and luck to figure out who they are and how good they are. And it's exasperating when they sit on your proposal for three months and then say no.'

These advisors of yours are entitled to their opinions. They have a right to be wrong. But if you are invested in the success of your book, politely ignore their advice.

During the six years I was writing and attempting to sell my first book, I listened to several of these 'wise, knowledgeable' people. That's part of the reason why it took me six years to sell my perfectly saleable book!

As I shall discuss in detail later, there are a few limited circumstances in which it might in fact be wise for you to proceed without an agent. But for most books and most authors, agents are invaluable. If you plan to take the time and care to do everything in your power to ensure that your book reaches its highest potential, finding an agent is the most important aspect of that time and that care. Putting yourself in the hands of a superb agent is worth whatever time and effort it requires.

In this chapter, I'm going to explain why you need a literary agent and tell you exactly how to get a good one.

WHY YOU NEED A GOOD LITERARY AGENT

1. An agent can often sell your book for a larger royalty advance than you would get if you were selling it on your own. And the bigger the royalty advance, the more effort the publisher is likely to put into promoting your book. So the agent, with all the valuable assistance he or she can give you, is in effect free, and will probably make you money in addition to paying his or her own way. (Most agents take 10 per cent of everything you ever make on your book.)
2. You are not a credible advocate for your own book. Of course you think it the best book ever written on your subject – you wrote it. But an editor knows that your agent has chosen to represent you out of hundreds of writers who approach her. Your agent's enthusiasm about your book carries weight. Her reputation for representing excellent books is important to her; in fact, it is her life.
3. An agent knows the publishing industry. He or she will select the houses and editors who should see your proposal based on information you can't hope to keep track of, no matter how many issues of *The Bookseller* you read.

   Good agents are friendly with many editors. They know who just got married, who loves sports, who made money in investments, who did their degree in psychology, who has a retarded child, who spent three years in Russia. They are on the inside track for information that might be critical for the best placement of your book, like who is about to buy out whom, what house just sacked its chief editor, or who just took on a hot new publicity director. An agent can make judgments about your book you can't begin to make because you lack the data.

   When I was wasting six years trying to sell my own book, I laboriously networked my way to an editor at one of the major publishing houses and felt triumphant when she agreed to read my manuscript. Shortly after that, I connected, finally, with my excellent agent. She wanted to show my project to a different editor at that house, but because one editor there had already turned it down, she couldn't. She later told me the editor I had found was the last person there she would have selected for my book.
4. An agent can apply many techniques and skills in selling your book that are unavailable to you. She may talk about a book for a

while before she actually sends the proposal out. She may find out if a similar book has sold in recent weeks or months. She may be able to get a little buzz going about your book, to make editors eager to see it. She knows exactly what to say in a cover letter that might excite an editor. She does far more to sell your book to the most appropriate editor and house than simply present it to a few editors.

5. As an individual, you have very little leverage in contract negotiations, for you have nothing that your publisher needs. Agents have bargaining chips: future books editors are thirsty for. They also have valuable experience and skill in negotiating publishing contracts.

6. After your agent has placed your book with the best possible editor at the best possible house and negotiated the best possible royalty advance and contract for you, he or she will try to sell any additional rights not sold to the publisher. These may include selling excerpts of your book to magazines (called 'serial rights'), audio rights, foreign rights, video, film, syndication and licencing rights. Remember that, unlike salaried rights representatives at a publishing house, agents make their living by the percentage they earn as a result of selling subsidiary rights. They have a vested interest in making sure that your book reaches as wide an audience in as many different forms as possible. This is why they are so keen to hold on to as many additional ('subsidiary') rights as they can when negotiating the initial contract for your book with the publisher who buys hardcover/paperback rights. Publishers will always try to buy all the rights ('world rights') in your book, but most agents will insist on retaining at least US and translation rights, together with any other rights (film, CD-ROM etc) that look likely to prove particularly lucrative.

These additional rights can add *substantially* to the revenues on your book, and it is all completely 'passive' income. Your agent does all the work; you need only wait for cheques to arrive in the post (unless you are invited to record the audio tape of your book in your own voice, or travel to a foreign country to promote your book abroad . . .).

7. When you run into conflicts or differences of opinion with your publisher, your agent will be a knowledgeable advocate for you. He will give you advice based on a great deal of previous experiences and will intervene on your behalf. This may sound

minor now, but when your publisher presents you with a jacket design you find appalling, or announces they are going to publish you in trade paperback rather than hardcover, you may find this to be the most valuable job your agent does for you.

8. Your agent will keep track for you of who owes you money and whether you are being paid on time. He will watch to be sure you are receiving your royalty statements on time, look for discrepancies in them, and interpret them for you, since many publishers still use royalty statements decipherable only to seasoned professionals.

9. A good agent (and that is the only kind you want) is a business and literary partner, an ally for you as you build your writing career. If your first book is successful, your agent will encourage and guide you and suggest next steps for you. If you continue to be successful, your agent will become as invested in your writing career as you are.

   When I completed my second relationship book, I gave my agent a proposal for a book on quite a different topic. She liked it, but strongly encouraged me to write instead a third relationship book, to build on my workshops, my reputation and my first two books. Only when I put my attention to it because of her suggestion did I discover my third book inside me, perhaps the most innovative of them all. I sometimes don't like what my agent has to say at first, but I've found that, virtually every time, she is right.

There are nine excellent reasons to take the time and effort necessary to hook up with a good literary agent. Of course I didn't even mention that major publishers often won't even look at unrepresented manuscripts. They put them in a pile that an assistant will go through six months from now if she ever gets the time. Just think how big that pile will be after six months' accumulation!

If you are serious about getting published, get an agent.

CHARACTERISTICS OF A GOOD LITERARY AGENT

1. By far the most important quality you are seeking in an agent is unmitigated enthusiasm about your book. You want an agent who loves your ideas and your writing and who shares your vision for your book. Usually an agent won't offer to work with you unless he or she is enthusiastic. But if an agent says, 'Well, I'll show it

around and see what happens,' don't leap on that offer. How can an agent who is unsure about the value of your work be an advocate for you?

2. Ideally, your agent will have a substantial track record of successful placements with major houses.

You might consider working with a new agent if it is a person who has extensive experience in some other phase of the publishing industry. Many agents are former editors, for example. But it is best not to go with someone who is a true beginner, or someone who for any reason cannot show you a substantial list of successful authors and publishing houses he or she has worked with. A lot of what you are paying your agent for is the experience you lack. Be sure you are getting what you pay for.

3. Your agent should be an aggressive negotiator and should believe in large royalty advances – unless money and large circulation is not one of your reasons for seeking publication.

Page's Postulate About Literary Agents is that there are two types of agents: those who don't believe in large royalty advances and those who do. The first kind will try to convince you that large advances are rare and that the average writer just can't expect to receive one. These agents want to be easy to work with, to keep editors happy and to sell lots of books, so when an editor offers a small advance, the agent encourages the author to accept it. Editors at publishing houses know that with certain agents, they can get away with a small advance for almost any book. And naive authors are grateful for the money, thinking that is the best they can do.

Agents in the second group are aggressive and always work to get the maximum amount for the books they represent. Editors know that when these agents show up, they mean business, and if they want a particular book, they have to be willing to pay well for it.

Maybe you yourself have a small to medium vision for your book. This is entirely appropriate for some books. Maybe you know your book has a specialised or small audience, or your goal in getting it published has nothing to do with earning money. Then, a Type I agent may be just right for you. But if you have a bigger vision for your book, either find a Type II agent, or be prepared to convince your agent to go for more money, a strategy I will discuss when we talk about the sale of your book in Step 10.

4. Your agent must be highly accessible.

Agents have many people wanting their attention all at once all the time. You want an agent who has a system for managing this problem other than not returning the calls of her own clients. It is inexcusable for your own agent to be hard for you to reach. Not only is it exasperating, it can often mean that you actually will not receive the services you are paying for.

Competent agents manage the problem in different ways. Some ask that you communicate by fax before you try to call. Some have excellent assistants who can meet some of your needs or put you through to your agent when the situation is urgent. Of course, you need to respect your agent's needs also, to call only when it's truly necessary, only during business hours, and to be understanding of the demands on his time. But you should always be able to reach your agent when you need him, consistently and reliably. Accessibility is part of what you are paying for.

While we are on the subject of accessibility, it is worth mentioning that the vast majority of agents – there are only a very few exceptions – are based in London. While you can handle most of your business with them by phone/fax/e-mail, it is likely that they will want actually to meet you at least once, if only to establish that you are as promotable in person as you claim to be in your proposal. So if you live outside London, be prepared to travel.

5. Ideally, you want an agent who is set up to sell US, foreign, serial, audio and other subsidiary rights. She should either be able to sell them herself, or have subagents who sell them for her. (See Steps 11 and 14 for more information on subsidiary rights.)

This is not an essential factor if everything else about the agent seems excellent. Often smaller literary agencies – some of which may be literally one-man or one-woman operations – will sell subsidiary rights to the publisher if they are not in a position to find buyers for some or all of these rights themselves. In this case, the publisher will attempt to sell these rights for you, and the agent will not be involved. The disadvantage of this arrangement is that the publisher will keep part of your royalties for subsidiary rights if they sell them. Often this is not a significant amount of money anyway. But if you believe that your book has major potential in US, foreign and other markets, look for an agent who manages her own subsidiary rights sales.

6. Ideally, your agent will be someone you like. Yours could be a close relationship and a long one. For periods of time it will become intense and even emotional. It would be wonderful if the whole experience could be enjoyable for you. But as is true with any relationship, you may not be able to get everything you want, and there are some elements in the relationship between you and your agent that are more important than others. For example:

    You need to respect your agent, to feel you are in competent hands and that you can trust the advice you receive.

    You need to feel your agent respects you and treats you accordingly.

    For most writers, it is less important that your agent be someone who will hold your hand when you experience disappointments. There is a lot of frustration and heartbreak in this business. Agents have to learn to weather it, and they like to work with clients who can be professional about the down times. Go elsewhere to cry and get angry, to express your frustration and to receive emotional support. Not that your agent won't be sympathetic. But don't expect him or her to be the one to listen and wipe your tears. Let your agent be the wise, professional mind you can return to when you are back together and ready to proceed.

    Don't insist that your agent have a personality that is perfectly matched to yours. If an agent is an aggressive negotiator who manages his time well, maybe he will be curt and businesslike with you on the phone sometimes. Maybe he will let you know when he becomes annoyed. If he is doing a good job for you, let minor irritations roll off your back.

7. What about a large vs. a small agency? Is there an advantage to either?

    No – apart from, possibly, where the selling of subsidiary rights is concerned. If an agent is a one- or two-person operation, be sure she is not overwhelmed all the time, that she answers her phone and is accessible. But those problems can exist with agents in large agencies too. Agents with clout and prestige abound in both categories.

So, to summarise, look for an agent who is enthusiastic about your work, experienced, aggressive, accessible, likeable and with whom you share mutual respect.

HOW TO FIND THE RIGHT AGENT FOR YOU

Back in my naive days, I used to ask people, 'How can I find a good agent?'

'Network,' people would tell me. 'Go to writers' conferences. Look in writers' reference books. Be positive and hope for the best.'

My primary motivation for writing this book was to take the vagueness, mystery and chance out of securing the services of a good literary agent and to offer instead an effective, systematic method. First you have to locate good agents, then you have to woo them, and finally, you need to screen them for the qualities you seek.

What my clients have come to call 'The Susan Page Method' of locating an agent has a number of advantages: It allows you to fling your net wide early on, so that you can find out *quickly* which agents have no interest in your work and identify several who do. Then, it allows you to send your proposal out for the first time to an agent *who has already expressed interest in it*. The Method gives you, the author, a great deal of control over the whole process, prevents you from having to wait months to hear from inefficient or inconsiderate agents, and, at the same time, honours agents' preferences for initial query letters and exclusive submissions – speaking of which, let me get this common question out of the way first.

EXCLUSIVE OR MULTIPLE SUBMISSIONS?

Many writers wonder why they should have to comply with the convention of sending their proposal to only one agent at a time, for this seems like it benefits agents and is a giant waste of time for writers. In fact, even though it may take a bit longer, exclusive submissions benefit you, the writer, too, in several important ways:

1. By submitting to one agent at a time, you are communicating to her that she is a top preference for you, and that you truly want to work with *her*. In your cover letter, you can convey your enthusiasm for her. For example, 'Susie Smith assures me that you are the best agent anyone could have.' Or 'Since you represent my favourite book, _____, I would like very much to work with you.' Or 'Because I know you have a special interest in animal rights, I feel you are the perfect agent for this book.' It is awkward to make statements like this if you also say, 'I am showing this proposal to several other agents at the same time.'

2. In your cover letter, you can write, 'Because I am giving you an exclusive look at this proposal, I would appreciate hearing from you within two weeks.'

3. While you are waiting to hear from this top choice, you can put 100 per cent of your hopes, desires, psychic energy and positive thinking into the one particular outcome you want most.

4. When you submit your whole proposal to several agents at once, you open the door for difficult decisions and awkward situations. Suppose your fifth favourite agent gets back to you immediately and says he is ready to go to work. But you haven't yet heard from choices one and two! What do you tell choice five? To wait a week or two and you'll get back to him? Not an auspicious beginning for an important relationship. Besides, suppose after five weeks, when numbers one to four have turned you down, number five just took on another book on your topic and is no longer interested in you?

5. As agents reject your proposal, sometimes they will tell you what they didn't like and offer you ideas that greatly strengthen it. If you are working with one agent at a time, you can incorporate the new ideas before you send your proposal out to the next agent. If you have already sent the proposal to five other agents, you may kick yourself that you can't now revise the proposal they are already reviewing.

6. If an agent asks you to make revisions in your proposal before agreeing to work with you, and you agree to make them, you may be in the middle of a relationship with one agent when a second one calls and agrees to take you on with no revisions. Now, you are receiving mixed messages about your work. You may feel confused and not know whom to believe or trust.

With The Method I suggest, you never have to be in the position of waiting longer than six weeks to hear from an agent before you can take further action if you choose to. Exclusive submissions keep you in control of the situation at all times and are more professional and beneficial for everyone involved than multiple submissions.

Here is The Susan Page Method for securing a literary agent:

1. SHOW YOUR COMPLETED, POLISHED PROPOSAL TO A PROFESSIONAL WRITER, EDITOR OR WRITING CONSULTANT

No matter how hard you have worked on your proposal and how many friends have told you it is fabulous, show it to a professional. In fact, if you can work with an editor as you are writing the proposal, even better.

An editor will suggest changes that can make the difference between a good proposal and a great one. Writing is a two-person job. You can never know what weaknesses you are failing to see. An experienced professional will know exactly what agents and editors look for in a proposal.

Agents reject more than 95 per cent of the proposals they receive. Yours has to be awesome to stand a chance of acceptance. Don't take a chance. And don't waste your chance submitting it to two or three superb agents just to find out that your idea is good but your proposal needs work. Be sure your proposal is in top shape before you ever send it out.

How do you find an editor or writing consultant? Here are several suggestions:

A. See if your local adult education college has classes on creative writing. Contact the teacher. He may be an excellent consultant himself, or may be able to help you find one.

B. Look in one of the magazines specially for writers, such as *Writers News* (available by subscription only) or *Writers' Monthly*. Their classified ads sections should include a number of advertisements from individuals offering editorial consultancy services. Most of these people will have worked as editors in publishing before turning freelance. As a rule they work by post and by phone/fax; they do not have to be based nearby.

C. *The Writers' and Artists' Yearbook* and *The Writer's Handbook* both list freelance editors.

D. Network with other writers, especially if you are in a writers' group or you have the opportunity to attend a writers' conference.

If possible, choose an editor who has worked specifically on book proposals. You want someone who is commercially aware, who will be able to judge whether your author, marketing, promotion and competitive books sections are strong enough to satisfy the demands of the current marketplace, as well as someone who can assess the merit of your book itself. Be sure to ask for and check references for every editor you contact.

Rates for this sort of work will vary from editor to editor. Some may charge per 1,000 words; some charge an hourly rate; some charge a flat fee. As a rule the more experienced the editor, the higher the fee. You will probably be able to get your proposal polished up for £200 to £400, more or less. Usually the editor will make suggestions about what the proposal needs, let you make the revisions, and then look over it again. If you want the editor to make the revisions, it may cost you a bit more.

Be sure to ask specifically for both 'concept' and 'copy' editing. You want your ideas to be well-organised and clearly presented, and you want your punctuation, grammar and style to be perfect.

Don't skip this step.

YOU MAY NOW SKIP TO STEP 5 IF . . .

. . . you already know that one agent is your top, top choice, because you know him, he represents the big book in your field, a friend raves about him or whatever. Only if he or she turns you down will you need to return to Step 2.

If you send a proposal without having first sent a query letter as described in Step 3, definitely say in your cover letter that this agent is your top choice and why. You may know of two or three agents you are certain you want to pursue, one at a time, without doing the query process first. This is a perfectly workable variation on The Method. However, if you don't have a *strong* preference for one or two particular agents, Steps 2 to 4 will be faster and are more likely to result in the best agent for your book.

2. CREATE A LIST OF AT LEAST TWELVE AGENTS YOU FEEL GOOD ABOUT

First, list the qualities and features you know you want in your agent, in the order of their importance to you. Consult the criteria I mentioned in the section above, 'Characteristics of a Good Literary Agent'. But only you know what your special needs and requirements are, so make your own list. Write it down.

Now, using the methods I suggest below, begin to create a list of agents who fulfil your criteria. Keep adding to it as you learn about agents who seem to be appropriate for you.

On the list, include everything you know about the agent: where you found the name, what books he or she has represented that you know of, any personal recommendations you received and so on.

If you still have only three or four agents on your list by the time you have completed your proposal, because you haven't had time to complete your networking and research, devote yourself to the list *full-time*. In two or three days, you can easily find twelve good names. You don't have to wait until you happen to blunder into an author; there are more effective methods.

METHODS FOR FINDING AGENTS

To find agents for your list, use one or more of these methods:

A. Go to a large bookshop to the section where your book will appear when it is published. Look in the Acknowledgments section of book after book to see if the author has thanked his or her agent. Write down the agent's name, the book and the author's comment. A simple thank-you is different from something like, 'I can't thank my wonderful agent enough for all he has done to enhance this book,' or whatever.

    Already now, you have agents on your list who represent your type of book and your subject matter, and you have some sense of how well-liked they were.

B. If there are books you especially respect whose agent is not mentioned in the Acknowledgments section, phone the rights department of the publisher. They will tell you the name of the agent for the book in question.

    But you may still want to contact the author to find out whether he or she felt good about working with that agent. Consider writing to the author. Sometimes, authors give their access information in the back of the book. Or write to the author care of the publisher. Here is a tip to make that effort more successful: Telephone the publisher first and ask for the specific editor of the book. You will probably reach an assistant or receptionist. Explain to the assistant that you plan to write to a certain author, and ask whether she will help you forward the letter and speed it as quickly as possible through the publisher's postroom. Maybe the assistant will let you address your letter directly to her, so that she can personally forward it immediately. (I devised this system after I received letters passed on from one of my former publishers four months after they had been written. But I have had great success in reaching authors with simple phone calls like this one.)

    Remember to enclose a stamped, self-addressed envelope with

your letter to the author (which should be as polite and compli-mentary as possible). The author will be doing you a favour in providing you with feedback on his or her agent – it's up to you to make that favour as painless as possible.

Most authors will, in fact, be happy to share with you the name of their agent and all their stories about working with him or her. This is a great way to network, meet a fellow author (who may even agree to endorse your proposal or book) and acquire some excellent information for your agent list.

C. Get hold of a couple of copies of *The Bookseller*, every edition of which contains stories about which agent has sold what exciting new book. These are usually agents who are currently 'hot', who negotiate good deals and are excellent at generating publicity. Select the ones who seem to be handling books like yours and write down everything the story tells you about them. Sometimes you will even learn how large an advance the agent was able to negotiate, and other juicy facts like this.

D. Go to the friendly independent booksellers with whom you are cultivating a relationship. Ask them to recommend agents. Though they have no reason to have regular contact with agents, they may know some just because they all run in the same circles. Remember, don't be content with the name. Ask the bookseller to tell you some-thing about the agent. See if you can pry out some revealing stories.

E. Contact the Association of Authors' Agents (it's probably best to make an initial approach by phone) and ask if they can send you a list of their members. Membership of this association is voluntary, but the agents who do belong meet minimum professional performance standards and must agree to abide by a code of practice. It is not a bad sign if an agent is not on this list. But you can be fairly certain that all of the agents who do appear on it are reputable. Members of the AAA must have been in business for more than three years; must earn an average commission of not less than £25,000 each year; and must agree to pay monies due to clients (from rights sales) within twenty-one days of receipt.

F. If you have the opportunity to attend a writers' conference, ask the published writers there to recommend agents. And of course, if you have any friends who are writers, ask them. Always remember to find out as much as you can about the agent. The Society of Authors and The Writers' Guild organise seminars which can be a useful source of gossip and information.

Now, using all the information you have gathered, list your agents in the order of your preference. Even the ones at the bottom of the list should be agents who meet all your basic criteria, so far as you can tell. Go to the library again and look up each of your agents in *The Writer's Handbook* or *The Writers' and Artists' Yearbook*. There you will find the accurate, current address and phone number for each of your agents.

3. CREATE A QUERY LETTER AND, ON THE SAME DAY, POST AN INDIVIDUALLY ADDRESSED VERSION TO EACH OF YOUR AGENTS

The 'query' is a one- or two-page letter that invites an agent to review your proposal and consider representing you. In most cases, a slight revision of the 'sell page' of your proposal will make an excellent query letter for a non-fiction book. For the fiction query letter, see Step 7. (The query letter is very different from the 'cover letter', also described in Step 7, that will accompany your actual proposal.)

Begin your non-fiction query with a sentence something like, 'I am seeking representation for my non-fiction book entitled, _____, for which I have a proposal and sample chapters.' Or 'I would like to invite you to review the proposal and sample chapters for my non-fiction book entitled, _____.'

If you were referred to this agent by someone he or she knows, mention that.

In a new paragraph, repeat the sizzling opener you used for your proposal overview, and continue with why there is a need for your book, how your book meets the need, how your book is distinctive from every other book and why you are the person to write the book. You may then want to add a short paragraph that summarises your table of contents or talks about how you will treat the subject.

But you must keep a query letter short; one page is best, two pages is maximum. The point of it is to save the agent time. Say only enough to make her eager to see more. If your proposal overview is two or more pages, you will need to abridge it for the query.

If the 'Market for the Book' and 'Promotion Plans' sections of your proposal contain extraordinary information, find a way to bring it into the query. (For example, 'I have a radio show,' or 'I speak to audiences of five hundred to three thousand at least five times every month.')

Do not say anything about previous unsuccessful attempts to find an agent or editor. After an agent expresses interest in you, that is the time to become honest with him or her about that.

Close your letter with this all-important sentence: 'I will show this proposal to only one agent at a time, so if you are interested in seeing it, please contact me immediately by phone, fax or e-mail.'

Since you are working with an editor to polish your proposal, let that person put finishing touches to your query letter too. Of course, be sure it is on a good-looking letterhead and is a beautiful, tidy presentation.

You may include one or two pages of supporting material with your query if you like, but not reams of material. Consider enclosing a couple of outstanding press clippings, a brochure about your speaking and workshops, a letter of endorsement from a well-known person or anything else that makes a very strong case for you or your subject matter. But enclosures are not necessary. Your book idea should be dazzling enough to speak for itself.

Even though you have invited agents to respond to you by phone, fax or e-mail, as a courtesy, include a self-addressed, stamped envelope with every query you send. Agents genuinely appreciate this and may be annoyed if you omit it.

Please note that I have said nothing about telephoning any agents. An initial phone call, 'Might you be interested in a proposal on blah, blah,' is a waste of time for both you and the agent. All he or she can tell you is, 'Send me something in writing.'

Post your query letter on the same day to a minimum of twelve agents – you may have more than twelve on your 'screened and qualified' list.

4. WAIT FOR RESPONSES

In most cases, if you have been following my suggested steps carefully so far, you will receive phone calls from one to possibly four or five agents within ten days or so, asking to see your proposal. (Of course, don't send your queries until you have your proposal completely ready to send.)

When you hear from an agent, thank him or her, say that you have received interest from several agents, and that you will be deciding within a few days which agent will receive the proposal first.

5. POST YOUR PROPOSAL TO ONE OF THE AGENTS WHO RESPONDED

Wait for a couple of weeks or so to allow all the agents who are going to respond to do so. Then, select one of the agents who responded and send him or her the proposal.

In a short cover letter, (a) thank him for his quick response to your query. (b) Assure him that he is the only agent reviewing the proposal at this time. (c) If you were referred to him by someone he knows, you will have mentioned this in your query but you might want to remind him again. (d) Show that you have done your homework and know something about him. Rave about another book he represents, or mention an interest you know he has or something about his reputation. (e) Say you hope to hear from him soon. That's about all the cover letter needs to say. Keep it short.

Remember to print or photocopy your proposal on one side only, and do not bind it. Simply put a rubber band around it or a large, squeeze-type paperclip. This makes it easier both to read and to copy.

On the outside of the envelope in red letters write, 'This is material you requested'. Be sure to use an envelope or package that is very easy for the agent to open. Five staples is enough on a padded envelope. Better still, use the kind that gives the recipient a rip cord to open it.

If you hear from several agents you like a lot, based on what you know about them so far, it can be hard to select the one to whom you will send the proposal first. Talk with the people who recommended the agents, review your notes, discuss with supportive friends and finally, just take the plunge and choose one.

Or, if several agents are *very* eager to see your proposal, you might consider reneging on your promise to do an exclusive submission. Go ahead and send the proposal to two, three or four agents, making it crystal-clear to all of them that you are showing your proposal to several agents at once. You may receive a faster response and work up a little frenzy about your proposal if agents know that they are competing with others. However, remember my remarks about the hazards of multiple submissions, and if you run into trouble, don't say I didn't warn you.

It is not necessary to respond right away to the other agents who called you, who won't receive the proposal first. If, after several weeks, your first choice turns you down, you will send the proposal to your second choice with a similar cover letter. When you finally seal a deal with one agent, it would be very thoughtful to send a note at that time to the other agents who responded to your query, thanking them for their interest and telling them that you have arranged to work with a different agent. You need not say which one.

6. PURSUE AGENT NUMBER ONE FOR SIX WEEKS

So, you have sent the proposal out to your first-choice agent. Now, wait three weeks. If you have heard nothing, phone the agency. If an assistant answers, speak to the assistant. Very sweetly ask whether she can tell you when you might expect to hear from the agent. If they give you a specific time frame that sounds reasonable to you, wait that long and, if you have heard nothing, call again. If they are vague about the time when you first call, wait another two weeks and call again. Never become indignant or angry on the phone, but do call. If the agent is hearing from you and not another author, she may move your proposal up in her pile.

Depending on how these phone calls go, make a decision whether to wait more or to move on. If the assistant assures you that your proposal has made it over the first hurdle and that you will hear soon, you may choose to be patient. But if you are hearing excuses, if the assistant or agent sounds irritated that you called, if they tell you that the agent is six weeks behind on her reading or that she's gone on holiday, you do have another choice.

7. AFTER SIX WEEKS OR SO, SEND OUT A SECOND PROPOSAL

If you have received no reassurances after six weeks, you may decide to fax or post the first agent a letter saying something like this:
   'Thank you for your interest in my proposal for _____. Since you have been unable to review it so far, I would like to allow another agent to see it. Unless I hear from you by Wednesday noon [give her one week], I will take the liberty of doing that. However, I do hope you are still interested in it and look forward very much to your positive response.'
   Wait a week to allow her to respond to this letter. If the agent is interested in your proposal, you will definitely hear from her. If you don't, then send the proposal to the second agent on your list.

In your cover letter to your second agent, you *must* tell her that this is not an exclusive submission. For example, 'Thank you so much for requesting to see the enclosed proposal for _____. I am showing it to you and only one other agent at this time, and I look forward very much to your response.'

Whenever you show your proposal to more than one agent at a time, always, *always* make it clear to all parties that you are doing so. This benefits both you and the agents. If an agent is truly interested in your proposal, knowing it is a multiple submission will force her to act quickly, which is to your benefit. Even more important, if an agent *thinks* she has an exclusive because you have not told her otherwise, she may spend time with your proposal before she calls you back, perhaps even to the point of suggesting revisions. You are both going to be upset when she calls you, eager to work with you and share her ideas, only to discover that you have already signed on with someone else. This situation leaves bad feelings all round.

A variation on this plan, if you like it better, is that you may ask an agent who has had your proposal for two months or more with no response to return your proposal. Include a large enough SAE with sufficient postage if you did not enclose one with the original proposal. The advantage of this alternative is that you can now send your proposal to a new agent as an exclusive submission.

8. WHAT TO DO WHEN AN AGENT REJECTS YOUR PROPOSAL

When an agent rejects your proposal, it will almost always be by post. Sometimes the agent will take the time to offer you specific comments and tell you why she decided to decline. Take her comments very seriously; they may give you a good idea for revising your proposal.

You may receive a standard rejection letter. This is understandable. Agents receive many, many proposals and can't spend very much of their time on people who are not yet clients.

If you receive a standard letter, call the agency back to see whether someone might be willing to give you specific feedback on your proposal. Often they will say no. However, they may have a page of notes relating to your proposal. Someone might be willing to take the time to read you those notes, or the agent may remember the proposal and take a minute or two to tell you why she rejected it. Sometimes agents' comments can be very helpful.

Often, agents will give standard reasons for not wanting to represent your book:

- The market is too crowded for books on your topic.
- It's a good idea, but only enough material for a magazine article.
- They have just taken on another book that is similar to yours.
- They are not taking on any new clients right now.

These are comments you don't need to take very seriously, unless you hear the same comment over and over again. Your proposal should already be strong enough to counter each of these objections.

When an agent rejects your proposal, you are allowed to be disappointed, sad, even angry – but not discouraged. Agents reject many, many proposals for reasons that have nothing to do with the saleability of the project or the quality of the work. All a 'no' means is that, for some reason known only to the agent, you didn't strike the right note. Remember that many successful books were rejected by numerous agents before they were sold. If the first agent you approach agrees to work with you, you are the exception, not the rule.

9. WHAT TO DO WHEN AN AGENT SUGGESTS REVISIONS

Often an agent will express interest in your idea but will suggest several changes in your proposal before agreeing to work with you. This is an excellent sign! Co-operate fully if you possibly can.

If the revisions being suggested take your work off in an entirely new direction, or they are changes with which you strongly disagree, you may have to decline. But if you can, work with the agent. In addition to wanting you to make the proposal into one she can get truly excited about, she wants to find out whether you are someone who is flexible, competent and easy to work with.

It's an awkward period of time. You are making changes, possibly time-consuming ones, for an agent who has not yet agreed to represent you. And she is spending time with you when she isn't sure you can produce what she wants. Treat it like a courtship. You may fear that you are not getting the unmitigated enthusiasm you seek. But an agent will not take time to suggest revisions in your proposal unless she is very interested in working with you. You'll be learning more about your potential agent and probably improving your proposal.

10. CONTINUE THESE STEPS UNTIL AN AGENT SAYS YES

Give the second agent the same six or seven weeks, calling at three- and five-week intervals, or whenever the agency has told you they would be in touch.

Continue working down the list of people who responded to your initial query.

If you need to compile a second list of agents, and send out a second batch of queries, go ahead and do that.

11. PERSEVERE

The difference between writers and authors is perseverance. It is the rare author who did not encounter obstacles, rejection, delays and all manner of exasperations before actually becoming published.

If you have tried your query on at least twenty agents and/or shown your proposal to at least ten, and you have received virtually no encouragement for your idea, then you may want to regroup. Go back to your proposal with a completely fresh mind. Is your idea original enough? Does your writing shine as much as it needs to? Maybe your organisational scheme lacks coherence or isn't conveyed well enough. Maybe your proposal doesn't distinguish itself sufficiently from other books on the market.

Possibly the most common reason agents and editors reject proposals is weak author credentials. Review the suggestions for enhancing your author credentials in Step 7.

You may decide that going this far was a good experience for you, but that you don't have the passion and determination to continue. Your real passions and talents lie elsewhere. This is a perfectly valid decision to make. Don't consider that you 'failed'. Realise that you succeeded in discovering one path that isn't yours. Congratulations! You can now be free for the rest of your life of the pressure to write a book!

Or you may be all the more determined to succeed. It is the world's problem that they aren't ready for your idea, not yours. You would be betraying yourself and your passion if you gave up now. Deep inside, you know your book will make an important contribution, and you will not be deterred by a few initial setbacks.

If that's true, congratulations to you too! Keep going. Find ways to strengthen your proposal. Get fresh ideas about it from new, wise and knowledgeable sources. Perhaps try working with a new editor. And then, just keep submitting it.

Always remember that many of the most popular and successful books in history were rejected numerous times before they were sold. Dr Seuss's first children's book, *And to Think That I Saw it on Mulberry Street* was rejected by twenty-seven publishers in the USA. The twenty-eighth publisher, Vangard Press, sold six million copies of the book. The bestseller *Chicken Soup for the Soul* was turned down by thirty-three publishers before the thirty-fourth picked it up. The book and its sequels have now sold more than eleven million copies and have been translated into twenty-five languages. Regarding the manuscript of *Anne Frank: The Diary of a Young Girl*, an editor wrote, 'The girl doesn't, it seems to me, have a special perception or feeling which would lift the book above the "curiosity" level.' One editor wrote to another after seeing the manuscript for *The Spy Who Came In from the Cold*, 'You are welcome to le Carré. He hasn't got any future.' And an editor told George Orwell regarding his manuscript for *Animal Farm*, 'It is impossible to sell animal stories.'

Statistics and stories like these would fill volumes. Agents and editors have widely divergent opinions, taste and judgments about the marketplace. If you believe in your project and you persevere with enough determination, you may very well proceed beyond numerous rejections and even insults to successful publication.

Perseverance is more likely to succeed with non-fiction than with fiction. General fiction that doesn't fit into any special genre, like romance, mystery or science fiction, is a great deal more difficult to sell than non-fiction. (See the Fiction Proposal section of Step 7.)

So don't give up. Pick yourself up after discouraging rejections and start again. Success will be all the sweeter when it comes.

12. WHAT TO DO WHEN AN AGENT SAYS YES

Usually, an agent who is interested in working with you will call you. It can be an exciting moment in your life! If you actually answer the phone, just remember to take a deep breath and contain your excitement enough to sound professional. After reading what follows, you will be ready for the phone call anyway. Enjoy it. If you receive a message to call the agent back, you may be a little more composed when you return the call.

You will be interviewing each other in this phone call. The agent may want to ask you some questions, but, if she is excited about your proposal, she may also be selling herself to you. Just go with the conversation, but be prepared ahead of time with a few questions, and at some point say, 'Do you mind if I ask you a couple of questions?' or just slip them in naturally.

At the time you send out a proposal, jot your questions for that agent down on a card and keep it with you, so it will be handy when she calls. Make your questions imaginative. What do you care most about in an agent? Ask about that. Look at the criteria listed earlier in this chapter. Which of them are most important to you? Tell your agent what your primary considerations are, and see how he or she responds. Don't be afraid to ask bold questions like, 'Do you consider yourself to be an aggressive agent? Would you say that you are easy to reach and stay in pretty close touch with your clients?'

Give this agent an opportunity to tell you an anecdote or two. For example, 'Do you find that there are conflicts between publishers and authors very often? What's an example of one you have resolved?' Or 'How did you get started as a literary agent?'

Ask whether he sells foreign and subsidiary rights himself, or whether subagents handle these for him.

There are also some questions you may want to avoid.

Don't ask what other books he has represented. Chances are your research has revealed the one or two that you care about. What you will hear is a string of titles you never heard of. Then you will have to act as if you *have* heard of them or else be embarrassed that you haven't. Later on, you can ask him to send you a client list, if you are very curious.

Don't ask what houses she has sold books to. Again, your research has revealed that she is experienced and competent, so she will have sold books to most of the major houses. The question will sound naive, as if you don't already know what a great agent you are speaking to.

Don't ask how large an advance she thinks she can get for your book. This question puts an agent on the spot at an early stage. She may be thinking that she can get £25,000 or £30,000 for it, but she will be reluctant to say so in case she doesn't end up with that figure.

You can certainly tell the agent what you would like to receive as an advance, but it's best to talk in round figures. Agents like terms like 'mid five figures'. Don't become too insistent in this initial conversation. However, if you know you are looking for an aggressive, high-advance-oriented, Type II agent, and you pick up a lot of Type I signals from this person, take careful note of this. Find out if you and this agent are on the same wavelength.

Most important in this initial conversation is to get a general sense of the agent's strengths and weaknesses with regard to your criteria, and to continue to convey, as you have in your proposal, great enthusiasm for your book. Repeat again, in different words, why and how this book is so important, why readers are going to love it, any evidence you have found since writing the proposal of the timeliness of your topic. See if you get the sense that the agent shares your enthusiasm. Tell him or her exactly what your vision for your book is, exactly what 'success' will look like for you. Stress that you already have lots of ideas for future projects, that you don't have just one book in you. See if this agent is behind you.

If there are parts of your publishing history you don't love, decide ahead of time exactly how much you want to tell your prospective agent in this initial conversation. For example, maybe your proposal has been rejected by several houses already, or you are already working with an agent you don't feel good about and are looking to switch. Maybe, if you decide not to work together, she never needs to know these things. If you do decide to work together, it is of course critical that you be fully open with her about everything very early on.

It is usually best not to agree to sign on with the agent in the initial phone call. He or she has made you an offer. This puts you in the driver's seat. Even though you may be very excited and enthusiastic, don't act precipitously. Take the time to think your decision through carefully. End the conversation by saying something like, 'I'm thrilled that you are interested in working with me and I have appreciated this conversation very much. I'm very, very interested in working with you, but I'd like to have a little time to think it over. I'll get back to you tomorrow or the next day.'

If you are already positive you adore this agent and working with her is your fondest dream come true, the delay may not be necessary. But don't hesitate to take it, especially if you have still not heard from other top agents on your list.

If you give yourself twenty-four hours, try to think through carefully all the pluses and minuses of this person. Do a little more research if you need to. Talk the whole thing over with people you trust, people who might think of something you forgot. Think through your first conversation. Most importantly, carefully consult your intuition, and see whether you have any hesitations or questions about this person. If so, you may want to discuss these further with the agent.

If, in your preliminary research, you have not already spoken with a current client of this agent, try very hard to do so now. The agent will probably be happy to provide you with one or two names or you may already have names from your previous research. You want to know what it is like to work with this person. This is a little tricky, because many agents have a few clients whose personalities don't match very well. If you happen to talk to one of those clients, you may get a skewed picture. Definitely consider the information you hear, but don't necessarily let one negative report deter you completely.

If for any reason you have ended up sending your proposal to more than one agent at a time, you may have 'first phone calls' with several agents who are eager to work with you. If you find yourself in this enviable position, it is ideal if you can meet each of the agents in person. This will give you a much better basis for making a decision. Even if you are considering only one agent, if it is possible to meet him or her in person, by all means do so.

After you complete all your research on the agent or agents who are courting you, and you make your decision, open the champagne. This is a great moment in your career.

Of course, there are variations on 'the first phone call'. Some agents will contact you initially by letter. When this happens, *you* initiate a phone conversation.

If the agent is too busy to talk to you, that is a clear indication of what your relationship will be like. But maybe this agent is absolutely perfect for your book, you know a lot about his or her reputation, and a businesslike, cordial relationship in which the communication is mostly by post and fax is just fine for you.

However it happens, when an agent agrees to work with you, *interview* him or her. Satisfy yourself that he or she meets your most important criteria.

Then *you* say yes, and you'll be on your way.

HOW TO GET AN AGENT TO FIND YOU

There is another way to hook up with an agent besides the systematic approach I've just suggested. Because it is less systematic, it is also less predictable, and you won't have as much control over the process. Nevertheless, especially for fiction writers, the other method might be faster, more direct and even more successful.

Most authors are chasing after agents. In the meantime, agents are chasing after an entirely different group of authors. Agents want to represent authors who are already successful writers or who have obvious talent just waiting to be bottled. So the question is, as my agent Sandra Dijkstra puts it, 'How can you become one of the chased (with an "ed")?'

Write book reviews or articles for national publications. In the byline, say, 'John Jones is working on a biography of Jack London,' or '. . . a novel about two families with triplets.' If an agent likes the review or article you wrote, he or she will wonder whether your book-in-progress is represented and may ask to see your manuscript.

Ask a prominent independent bookseller to look at some of your writing. If you receive an enthusiastic response, ask whether that person might recommend you to an agent.

If you know that your creative writing teacher loves your work, see whether he or she might be willing to rave about you to an agent who is a friend or an acquaintance.

Enter national writing competitions for unpublished writers and win prizes. Details of these competitions are given in *The Writer's Handbook* and *The Writers' and Artists' Yearbook*.

If you should ever find yourself at the centre of something particularly newsworthy – like one of those 'human interest' stories or scandals that make it on to national television and newspaper front pages – agents will be beating a path to your door. As a rule, these events aren't something you can pre-arrange; but make the most of them if they happen to you.

In other words, find ways to get yourself and your writing noticed or to have credible people praise your work in the right circles. If your writing is truly excellent, this may put you into that enviable group of authors who are 'chased'!

THE AGENCY AGREEMENT

Literary agency contracts or letters of agreement are usually fairly short – one to five pages – and straightforward. They describe what the agent will do for you, how he or she will be compensated, how disputes will be settled, and how either of you may terminate the agreement.

Most agents these days receive 10 per cent (plus VAT) of all proceeds from your royalties and sub-rights sales on anything they sell or manage for you. However, some agents are now asking for 15 per cent or even more as standard. This percentage should include administration charges and the cost of any work the agent herself does on your proposal or manuscript – although some additional admin costs, such as photocopying, may be extra.

You should make sure that the contract clearly defines the agent's area of responsibility. Will the agent expect to handle any other work you might undertake – journalism, or radio and TV, for example? Will the agent demand to receive a percentage of any earnings on deals that you yourself negotiate? The agent could argue that such deals and offers are a direct result of the success that she has engineered for you as a result of the work she has done on your behalf. And she has a point. This is a grey area, but one which you should clarify.

The contract usually provides that you will work with your agent exclusively, but that either of you may terminate your agreement with thirty to ninety days' written notice.

I have rarely come across an author who felt the need to change anything in the agency agreement before signing it, or who lived to regret any of the provisions. Nevertheless, read it very carefully several times. If you feel that you need to seek a professional opinion, the Society of Authors and the Writers' Guild provide excellent contract vetting services (though you do have to be a member).

PROPOSAL REVISIONS

Very often, an agent will suggest revisions in your proposal after you agree to work together. Co-operate fully, unless you simply can't live with the requested changes. Even though you may disagree at first, you will be amazed at how often agents are right. And the proposal must be something the agent can represent without reservation, with great enthusiasm and conviction.

One more comment: As you work with your agent and develop an ongoing relationship, decide on the way to communicate with her that works best for both of you. When things are really happening with your proposal, you may be on the phone to each other often. But when you have a question or a need that is not urgent, sometimes the best plan is to fax her a memo so she can get back to you at her convenience. If you hear nothing for a couple of days, then you can follow up by phone. Always have respect for her needs at the same time as you stand up for your own.

And don't forget to thank her, often. She is making a big difference to your life.

For information about how to switch to a new agent if you ever feel the need, see Step 20.

CIRCUMSTANCES WHEN YOU MIGHT WANT TO PROCEED WITHOUT AN AGENT

If you have tried the above method and have been unsuccessful in wooing an agent, but you still believe very much in your book, you may want to look for interested editors on your own. It could be that agents are not interested in your book, not because it doesn't have merit, but because they do not see it as a big 'commercial' book, a book that will make enough money to be worth their time. This is not to say that your book is not capable of making money, nor is it to say that no publishers will be interested in seeing your work.

Research the market. Find our which publishers might be particularly suitable recipients of your proposal. Draw up a list of publishing houses who publish in your area of expertise, and target them individually, in just the same way that you might target an agent – by sending out a query letter and then, if you get a positive response, a proposal. Although it's true that many of the larger publishing houses will look less favourably on unagented work and consign it immediately to their 'slush pile', others welcome approaches from unagented authors.

If you are entrepreneurial and believe you would enjoy serving as your own agent, and you have the time and skills required to do an excellent job for yourself, you might choose to proceed on your own. You can find ways of selling your book to publishers that are every bit as creative and forceful as methods used by an agent. One word of caution: if you do receive an offer from a publishing house, check it out thoroughly to make sure that you are getting the best possible deal. The two writers' unions (the Society of Authors and the Writers' Guild) have negotiated a Minimum Terms Agreement (MTA) to which a number of publishing houses have signed up. Even if your potential publisher hasn't, the Agreement makes a useful benchmark against which you can judge the contractual terms you are being offered. The MTA is available free of charge to members of the Society of Authors and the Writers' Guild (send an SAE).

✳   ✳   ✳

That's my version of the story on agents. Proceed carefully, with patience and persistence. This is an important relationship. Don't settle for less than what you want.

Sell Your Book

If you have properly completed Steps 1 to 9, Step 10 will consist of two parts:

1. Wait for the phone to ring.
2. Open the champagne.

Well, it's almost that easy. There might be a few conversations with your agent before you actually start the celebration. But the point is, your agent does all the work.

When you and your agent have altered your proposal, if she suggested changes, so that it satisfies you both, she will ask you to duplicate it or she will duplicate it herself, possibly at your expense. Then, she will show it to a handpicked group of editors, selected on the basis of their compatibility with your topic, at a handpicked group of publishing houses. Within somewhere from two to ten weeks, she will receive either no offers to buy it, one offer or several offers.

REJECTIONS

Let's talk about the rejections first. Tell your agent ahead of time whether or not you want to be told as editors reject your work. You have the option of waiting until either one says yes or they all say no, and only then hearing all the gory details of what went on before. Or you may want to stay up to date and hear about every communication as it occurs.

In either case, at some point, ask your agent for copies of all the rejection letters. Some will make you angry, some will make you cry, and some will make you laugh. But you will learn by reading them. If you see the same piece of feedback twice, you may want to pay attention to it. Even if the comments are wrong, like, 'There is no market for this at this time,' when you know of a book on the topic or in your genre that just sold 50,000 copies, you are hearing the prevailing industry wisdom. Now you know what you will have to overcome if you are to succeed.

If your agent receives no offers on his first round, this will be disappointing, but it is not uncommon. You and your agent will discuss what to do next. Usually, he will submit it to a second round of editors. If he has no success there, you will have to strategise. Maybe there is a way you can change the focus or broaden the audience for the book. If you change the proposal substantially, the agent may, at his discretion, be able to show it to some editors again.

Is there anything you can do after two rounds of rejection? Of course.

You can substantially revise your proposal.

You can make certain your agent has shown the book to every house that is even a remote possibility. I once worked with a man whose agent could not sell his book. Nine months later, he had networked his way to a small publisher who was interested in it, and had almost sealed a deal with them, when his agent called to say she was having lunch with an editor from a major publisher and mentioned his book and the editor was very much interested. We couldn't believe she had not already approached this publisher! They did sell the book to this new editor.

The other thing you can do is start exploring small presses on your own. Review my comments about small presses at the end of Step 5. Start browsing and see if you find one that looks right for your book. You may ask your agent to approach them, or you may do it on your own. If you place your book on your own with a small press, you may want to discontinue the relationship with the agent. Your letter of agreement with her will tell you how to do this; usually, you'll give thirty to ninety days' written notice. As small presses generally pay very small advances, your agent shouldn't object too strongly.

REQUESTS FOR ADDITIONAL INFORMATION

Often, one or more editors will ask your agent for additional information before making a decision. They may want to meet you in person to assure themselves that you are someone who can promote your own book. Although this may mean forking out the price of a train ticket, go! This is a fabulous opportunity for you to display your enthusiasm for your book – and your commitment to it.

A prospective editor may at least want to talk to you on the phone. If you have video footage available of yourself giving a speech or TV appearance, or even an audio tape, the editor will want to see that.

You might have conversations, not only with the editor who is considering acquiring your book, but also with people in the marketing, sales and publicity departments as well.

Whether you speak to them on the phone or in person, prepare yourself ahead of time for your interviews with editors and marketing people. Anticipate what you might be asked and prepare answers. Of course you will want to seem natural and unrehearsed, but don't assume that, just because you know your material, you don't need to think ahead about this interview. Be prepared to talk enthusiastically, not only about the subject matter in your book, but also about any special plans you have for marketing and promoting the book yourself.

Before I sold my first book, *If I'm So Wonderful, Why Am I Still Single?*, I flew to New York to visit several publishing houses who had indicated an interest in the book. For my very first interview ever, I was seated at a conference table with seven or eight people from a variety of departments. Someone asked me what singles were complaining most about these days. Even though I was regularly conducting workshops for singles and had written a complete book about the whole scene, I had no idea how to answer this question. It was a little like the question, 'Tell me about yourself.' The editors and publicists did not get the picture of someone who can think quickly and be spontaneous. I got my act together a bit more for subsequent interviews, and was not surprised to learn later that the first publishers were not among those who made an offer for the book.

If you are given the opportunity to speak to publishers before the sale of your book, look over Section Five of Step 18 where I give you tips for media interviews. Most of those tips will be useful for your interviews with editors too. After all, one of the main qualities they hope to see in you is the ability to 'come across' in demanding situations.

ONE OFFER

Often, your agent will receive one offer from an editor. Your agent will call you, and the two of you will discuss whether or not to accept it. Most often, your answer will be yes.

However, if you have reason to believe that your book is worth more than this offer, you can suggest that the agent ask for more money. Or you can turn down the offer. If the publishers really want the book, they may come back with a larger offer. But this is a very tricky call, because it could leave you with no publisher at all.

This is a situation in which your agent will be a great help to you. He or she will be able to judge whether the offer is a reasonable one, or what your chances might be if you try again. If you feel your agent could be more aggressive, don't hesitate to encourage him or her. Send a fax in which you substantiate your reasons for believing the offer is too low.

Accept, negotiate some more, or try again elsewhere. Those are your options when you receive a single offer.

Most often, the offer will be appropriate for the book, you will accept it, with perhaps a little fine-tuning of terms and conditions, and you will be on your way. Congratulations! You are launched!

MULTIPLE OFFERS

If it turns out that two or more editors express an interest in buying your book, this is the best of all possible worlds. Then, your agent will hold an auction.

Auctions take place over the phone. The agent sends out a letter to the interested parties in which she establishes the date and ground rules for the auction.

Sometimes, an editor who is very eager will make a preemptive bid, that is, he or she will try to get you to accept an offer before the auction takes place. If this bid is larger than the agent thinks the final bid in an auction would be, or if this house is especially perfect for this book, or if the editor is someone with a fabulous reputation who has the perfect vision for your book or has promised a large promotion budget, or if the agent knows of some other special circumstance, your agent may advise you to accept the preempt. Otherwise, she'll suggest you turn down the preempt and go ahead with the auction.

Sometimes, an editor will try to persuade you and your agent to accept a 'floor' for the auction. A floor is a minimum bid, the amount at which the auction will begin. But, as protocol has it, the house that establishes the floor retains the privilege of topping the highest bid by 10 per cent. A floor puts all the other bidders at a serious disadvantage. They may bid their hearts out and their budgets up and still lose in the end because, no matter what they bid, the house with the floor agreement can sweep in at the end and top whatever they have offered.

Often, an agent will suggest that you refuse to accept a floor, because it discourages other bidders. But when a house offers one, the agent can then tell other houses that she has turned down a floor, and she can state the amount. This will start to create a buzz about your book and build the excitement, something a good agent will be adept at doing.

Your agent might advise you to accept a floor if it comes from a house she is certain would be right for your book, and the floor is high enough so that if no other bids come in, you will still be happy. A publisher might bid, even if another house has established a floor, if they think the floor is close to the top bid of the house that offered it, and they know they can bid more. The decision about whether or not to accept a floor is a delicate one. If your agent has a strong inclination, you are probably well-advised to follow it. But don't hesitate to discuss it with her until you understand all the ramifications.

At the pre-established time, the auction begins. Editors phone in their bids. Then the agent calls them all back, reports the results of the first round and accepts a second round of bids. Finally, after several hours, or occasionally even several days, all the editors but one have dropped out, and the highest bidder, or the editor with the best overall package, wins. Agents and authors often reserve the right not to sell to the highest bidder; they may want to consider other critical criteria like the reputation of the editor, the appropriateness of the house for this book, the promotion budget, other terms in the offer, and so on. Then your agent calls you, tells you the happy news, discusses any loose ends and advises you to accept.

Congratulations! Throw a big party! Thank all the loyal friends and relatives who have supported you through the early phases of this project.

THE ROYALTY ADVANCE

Now we come to the delicate matter of discussing the size of the royalty advance. How much can you reasonably expect to receive up front when you sell your book?

It depends.

It depends on everything from your subject and your credentials to the perceived market for your book, from the agent who is representing you to the state of the economy at the time of the sale, from the format of the potential book (hardcover or paperback) or how well other books like it have done in the marketplace recently.

First, a little background information.

The amount you will earn on each book sold will be determined in your contract. These amounts are usually fairly standard: for a hardcover, this could mean 10 per cent of the published price to 4,000 copies sold, 12½ per cent to 7,500 copies sold and 15 per cent after. If the publisher decides to reprint a small quantity of your book after the initial print run has sold out, the royalty may revert to 10 per cent. So if your hardcover sells at, for example, £16.99, you will receive between £1.69 and £2.54 on each copy sold.

On mass market paperback sales, your royalty will usually be 7½ per cent of the published price to 30,000 copies sold and 10 per cent after. You will therefore receive between 45p and 59p on each copy sold on a mass market paperback selling at £5.99. The royalty rate is lower because the margin of profit is obviously much smaller for the publisher on each book.

Now back to the size of your advance.

Generally, the royalty advance is an estimate of the number of books the publisher thinks can be sold in the first year or so of the book's life. This will depend on whether the book is to be published in hardcover or in paperback; the estimate can also be reasonably based on the previous sales record of similar books.

If the last three paperback books on a particular theme each sold approximately 20,000 copies in the first year or so, it is a reasonable guess that your new book on the same subject will sell at roughly the same level. If, therefore, your royalty scale says that you will get a 7½ per cent royalty on each book sold at £5.99 (about 45p per book), then the publishers will pay you 45p × 20,000 = £9,000.

On books for which a previous track record of similar titles (or books by the same author) isn't relevant, excitement and speculation start to play a role.

I have seen authors accept what I thought was far too small an advance for their books, because they had no way of knowing that a larger advance was even a possibility. Some of these people were agented – represented by non-aggressive, Type I agents, who let the low offered advance stand.

But I have also seen authors who had their hearts set on a £50,000 advance bitterly disappointed with £20,000, which was in fact a more than fair advance for that book.

I would love to be able to spare you either scenario.

Let me tell you two stories.

A woman I know, Diane, wrote a proposal for a book on a general self-help subject about which she felt very passionate. A major publishing house offered her £5,000 for it. She honestly believed it was worth more than that and, through her agent, turned it down. The publisher came back with an offer of £7,000. Diane still said no. She was courageous to turn down a 'bird in the hand' like this, but she and her agent had a strong conviction that these offers were not adequate.

Next, the publisher asked Diane what she would accept to do the book.

'Twelve thousand pounds,' she replied. She nearly fainted when her agent called her back and said, 'You've got it.'

Moral: As long as you believe it is reasonable, and have a factual basis for your belief based on all the information you can gather, stand up for what you want. If your conviction is strong, put courage behind it.

On the other hand, be prepared to accept less than your highest fantasy for a book. And don't count your chickens before they hatch!

Another friend, Michael, had the opposite experience from Diane's. Someone he knew had received a large advance for her book, over £50,000. Michael's book idea was similar enough in nature for him to be certain that he too could earn a big advance. He gave up his day job and threw himself into his writing. But because of the particular slant of his book, it was viewed by the publisher as a different category, one that had a more modest sales history. The most he could get for his book was £15,000.

He had to endure not only disappointment but some financial hardship, though he did write a wonderful book that became quite successful and launched him into a new business that he now loves.

Royalty advances are not an exact science. All I can say is, don't settle for one that you know is too low, and don't be greedy. Where those parameters fall for your book, you will have to work out for yourself.

THE 'SIX-FIGURE ADVANCE'

So what about the coveted 'six-figure advance'? Some writers do receive big money for their books. Might you?

Here's a little test. If you write non-fiction, your book might possibly have the potential to earn a six-figure royalty advance if:

1. Your book is on a topic of wide general interest that could excite a large number of readers.
2. Your book has a distinctive angle and makes an original contribution to its field. It doesn't have to have new information; your book can be distinctive in its presentation, in its vocabulary, in its imagery, or in the specific sub-topic of the general topic that you emphasise.
3. You have substantial credentials to write on this topic, OR you have a co-author who does, OR you can get an extremely famous person to write a foreword for you.
4. You have prepared an extraordinary proposal by following the outline in this book, and you are working with a competent editor to perfect the final product.
5. You have a show-stopping title.
6. You secure the services of an experienced, well-known literary agent who loves your book and who believes it has the potential to earn a six-figure advance.
7. You are both willing and able to promote your book on radio and TV and in print media. Editors may want to meet you or see videotapes of you to assure themselves that you have an appealing personality and are as articulate and enthusiastic about your topic in person as you are in print.

These seven ingredients don't guarantee a six-figure advance by any means, but if any one of them is missing, your chances of receiving one are greatly diminished. Jumping through these seven hoops is necessary – but not sufficient.

With fiction, the criteria for a six-figure advance are fewer, and subjective judgments play a larger role. Your fiction book has the potential to earn a six-figure advance if:

1. Your story is built around a topic that is of widespread interest or that has the potential to spark interest in many readers.
2. The quality of your writing is superb, perhaps even has a distinctive character or voice.

3. You have an experienced and influential literary agent who loves your work and is fully committed to you, your writing and your career.

Of course, if you are already a celebrity of any kind, as many best-selling authors are, you can bypass all of this and write your own ticket.

One last thing to keep in mind when you are negotiating your advance: Although publishers are paying you up front to write your book, they do not base their advance amount on what you will need in order to survive while you write; they base it on what they think your book will earn. If you are trying to boost the size of your advance, don't use arguments with the publisher about your financial status; it's of little concern to them. Use arguments about the extra-ordinary potential of your book to make money for them!

There are exceptions to this: An agent may decide it is strategic when dealing with a particular editor to refer to your needs at some point. And your finances will become relevant if extensive travel or research will be necessary to complete your book. The publisher may want to help pay for all or part of that, but it is still calculated as a part of the royalty advance.

THE PAYMENT PLAN

The schedule of payments according to which you will receive your royalty advance is quite negotiable.

It is customary for the publisher to pay you half of your advance when you sign your contract and the other half on publication. For larger advances, the publisher may want to pay you one-third of your advance when you sign the contract, one-third when your manuscript is accepted, and the final third on the book's publication date, or twelve months after your manuscript is accepted, whichever comes sooner. It is also common for publishers to pay a quarter or a third of the advance when the deal is made and another portion upon delivery of a partial manuscript so that they can evaluate the book's progress. But variations on these schedules are quite common. If you want one, ask for it.

Look at your own financial situation and figure out what you would most like as a payment schedule. Don't forget to think about taxes. Sometimes it will be to your advantage to delay a substantial payment until the next tax year. Then, tell your agent what you would like and ask her to request it.

＊   ＊   ＊

Now that you are armed with this information, you'll see that what you need most to sell your book successfully is trust in your agent. I hope you are now convinced that the selection of an agent you genuinely respect and like is worth whatever time and effort it requires. Sometimes your agent will be guiding you through delicate, momentous decisions. By the time you have sold your book, you will know each other much better. I hope you are both happy with your decision to work together.

Negotiate and Sign
Your Contract

*Time required: Four to six hours of work plus
one or two hours of phone calls over several weeks.*

Wow! You sold a book! You are an author! Your huge cheque should arrive this week, shouldn't it?

Well, not this week.

Probably not for about two or three months. And then, expect to receive a third to a half of the total you negotiated. As we saw when we discussed the payment schedule of the contract, you don't get it all at once.

Here's how it goes:

About one to two months after you seal the deal with a publisher, you will receive a draft of your contract. You'll study it as I explain below, and you and your agent will negotiate the fine points and send it back to the publisher.

In another month, you will receive the revised contract. Usually, everything will be in order. You will sign and return three copies: one for you, one for your agent and one for your publisher.

Now, in another one to three weeks, you will receive your copy signed by the publisher and, soon after, a cheque from your agent, with her 10 per cent already extracted. It won't be for the full amount of the royalty advance, but the portion you will have agreed at the time of the sale to receive at this time, usually one-third to one-half of the full amount.

WHY IT TAKES SO LONG TO RECEIVE YOUR CONTRACT
AND YOUR MONEY

It is usually at least three months from the sale of your book to the signing of the contract and your receipt of the cheque. So why does the contract process take so long?

Your editor has to originate a contract request that often has to circulate through the publishing house and be approved by a number of people including the editorial director, the publisher and the financial manager. It could be delayed for several days on any of their desks while they are away on holiday or busy with other tasks.

The contracts department, which has the task of actually drawing up your contract, very often becomes backlogged. Your contract request may sit in someone's in-tray for several weeks before it gets formally drawn up.

After you receive a first draft of the contract and you or your agent ask for certain changes, negotiations may take several weeks while various people at the publishing house discuss them. Then, when both parties are happy with the contract, it has to go back to the contracts department again to be revised, to the publisher or editorial director for signature, and back to your agent for your signature.

Then there is the cheque run. Cheques at the publishing house may be generated only once a month. If the signed contract reaches the contracts department the day after cheque-writing day, another month goes by before the cheque gets written.

In short, be assured that your contract is not simply sitting in one person's in-tray for three months – the scenario I had envisaged. Instead, people you may never meet are giving their time and attention to your book. Be flattered, and be patient.

DON'T WAIT FOR YOUR CONTRACT
TO START WRITING YOUR BOOK!

By the time you sign your finalised contract, you should be well into the heart of your project. As I am writing this today – Step 11 of 20 steps – I have only just received the *draft* of my contract for this book. By the time I receive the first portion of my advance, I may have most of the first draft of this book complete.

Of course, I have an early delivery date for the manuscript and am writing full-time. But even if you have only a few hours a week to work on your book and your delivery date is twelve or eighteen months away, start your writing schedule now. Keep up the momentum you have begun by writing your proposal. If you take a break until you receive your signed contract, you may have a much harder time gathering up the energy to begin your project again.

REVIEWING YOUR CONTRACT

Your agent is an expert at book contracts. Her job is to scrutinise each clause and to negotiate everything she can in your favour. Because she is a specialist in this area, it is highly unlikely that you will need the services of a solicitor (unless there are special complications). Remember that the Society of Authors and the Writers' Guild offer contract vetting as a member service. If you have a contract in hand, ready to be reviewed, you can apply for Associate Membership of these organisations even if you have never been published before. You'll find more details about this in the Resources section.

Some writers trust their agent implicitly and leave everything up to them. This is, of course, an option for you too. However, I believe that the few hours it will take you to familiarise yourself with your contract is well worth the time it takes. Studying the contract will make you more confident of your rights and expectations and will give you more control over your own destiny. Compare the terms and conditions of your contract with those laid down in the Minimum Terms Agreement (see Step 9) – remembering, of course, that not all publishers adhere to the MTA and that some publishers will be determined to stick to their standard terms no matter what. If you and your agent feel that your contract offers you a fair deal overall, you may be happy to go along with their suggestions.

In the margins of your draft or on a separate piece of paper, make a note (in pencil, if on the contract itself) of every tiny detail that you don't understand and everything you would like to improve. Then, in a conversation with your agent, ask her about every item you've noted. She will explain the details where they are not clear to you, fill you in on the general practices of the publishing industry, and make a note of everything you want her to ask about in her next conversation with the publisher.

Ask for everything you want. Sometimes the agent will say, 'I can ask, but I've never seen a contract with that provision, and I'm sure the publisher won't agree.' If you feel strongly about it, persist. If you and she mount a strong enough campaign, you have good reasons for what you are requesting, and you are dealing with fair-minded people at the publisher's end, maybe your wish will be granted. (If you are asking for something unconventional, let's hope you have a Type II agent.)

It is probably sensible to limit your requests to issues that really matter to you. You will be taken more seriously if you ask for only one or two major changes.

The following list of items to watch out for is not exhaustive. What I discuss here are several of the most negotiable, controversial, or interesting clauses which you will encounter in your contract.

ROYALTY ADVANCE, ROYALTIES AND PAYMENT SCHEDULE

These will have been negotiated when the sale was made and are usually not open for further discussion at this stage. A deal is a deal. In addition, you should bear in mind that publishing is a low-margin-of-profit business that depends on volume of sales. To make serious money, you need to sell lots of copies of your book. You can help enormously with this by writing the best book possible and then devoting all your energies to promoting it.

Sometimes you might be able to alter the number of sales at which your royalty percentage increases, or establish a sliding royalty scale if none already exists. But these negotiations really should have been completed at the point of the initial offer.

SUBSIDIARY RIGHTS

Again, the assignment of these rights should have been decided when the deal was made. As you've already learned, an experienced, competent agent will probably encourage you to keep control of as many rights as possible, rather than selling world rights to the publisher, because then your agent will be able to make you extra money from each new subsidiary rights sale. But all rights are highly negotiable.

US AND TRANSLATION RIGHTS

These rights can be extremely lucrative. Agents usually hold on to these rights on your behalf; however, if they have been assigned to the publisher, then the publisher should pay you a higher initial advance than if they are buying UK rights only.

For example, let's say your publisher pays you £20,000 for the right to publish and market your book in the UK. If you and your agent then sell the book to a US publisher for another £10,000, and make translation rights sales in three or four countries for a total of £8,000, then you've earned a total advance of £38,000.

However, if your publisher buys world rights, the Minimum Terms Agreement recommends that they can retain 15 per cent of the proceeds of any US rights sale and 20 per cent of the proceeds of any translation rights sale. You are therefore losing, potentially, £1,500 on the US deal and £1,600 on the translation rights sales. This means that your advance will be more than £3,000 lower. You won't see any money that your publisher makes from these deals as hard cash. Your publisher will set your share of the monies against the royalty advance they have already paid you, if the earnings of the book have not yet covered this (if the book has not 'earned out' its advance). This means that, if you have good foreign sales, you will earn out your advance and begin earning royalties over and above your advance sooner. But, clearly, in this instance, the original advance offered by the UK publisher should be higher to take the world rights assignment into account.

Most agents will be very keen to hang on to US rights. But translation rights may be a bargaining chip that you will choose to relinquish in favour of something you value more.

SERIAL RIGHTS

There are two different sorts of serial rights: first serial rights, which means a newspaper or magazine has the right to reprint extracts from your book before it is published; and second serial rights, which give the press the right to reprint extracts from your book after it is published. First serial rights are obviously more desirable as far as the media are concerned, because if they buy these they then have 'an exclusive', as no one else is yet able to read your book.

If your publisher buys first serial rights, you should receive 90 per cent of the proceeds from any sale; the percentage will be less than this for second serial rights.

You should also receive 90 per cent of the proceeds for the following rights sales made by your publisher: TV and radio dramatisations, film rights and dramatic rights. For the right to quote from your work in an anthology or quotation, you should receive not less than 50 per cent; for the sale of merchandising rights, 80 per cent; and for sound and video recording rights, not less than 75 per cent. Electronic rights, including the right to turn your book into a CD-ROM, are becoming more and more important, particularly for certain types of non-fiction. Until recently clauses encompassing these rights were omitted altogether from many contracts, but they are now becoming standard. Try to negotiate the best percentage you can if you think that your book has CD-ROM potential.

Whatever rights your publisher (or your agent, for that matter) sells on your behalf, they should seek your consent in writing before accepting the deal.

BOOK CLUBS

It is usual for publishers to buy these rights as they tend to have closer relationships with the book clubs than agents. When book clubs buy the right to sell a book through mail order (often in a special edition with a different format), they usually do so at a 'royalty inclusive' price; that is to say, they agree beforehand how many copies they will buy from a publisher and pay a set amount of money per copy. In this case, you should receive at least 10 per cent of the publisher's receipts. On a 'royalty exclusive' deal, when royalties are paid on sales in the usual way, you should receive at least 50 per cent of receipts.

REPRINT RIGHTS

The publisher almost always retains 'reprint' rights – the right to reprint a hardcover book in a paperback format.

Usually about a year after a hardcover is published, the potential market for that relatively expensive format has been saturated and the publisher is keen to get it into the cheaper paperback format so it will reach a wider audience. Going into paperback should also give your book a new burst of publicity.

Increasingly publishers are opting for what is known as 'vertical' publishing, which means that they will pay a higher initial advance for the book in the knowledge that they are going to publish in both hardcover and paperback. In the past it was common for hardcover publishers to sell the paperback rights to a different publisher; however, this is becoming much less usual and most publishers now choose the vertical option.

DELIVERY DATE

The publisher will probably suggest a date by which you must deliver your completed manuscript. Agree only to what you feel is feasible. A good rule of thumb is to estimate how long you think it will take you to complete your book *and then add three months to that time*. It detracts from the pleasure of writing your book if you always feel rushed, and you are unlikely to produce your best work. And things happen in life which cannot always be foreseen. Set a time that seems comfortable to you and refuse to be budged.

On the other hand, your publisher may tell you that there are important marketing reasons to publish a book in a certain month and may put pressure on you to accept a less leisurely delivery date. Take this into consideration, but don't set a delivery date that is going to ruin your life for the next few months.

Most of us loathe deadlines but, if we didn't have them, very few books would ever get written.

PERMISSIONS

If you plan to quote or reprint copyrighted material from other sources, you will have to 'clear rights' in that material before publication with the owner of the copyright, which is usually done via the publisher of the source from which it is taken. Depending on where your book is going to be available in the world, you will have to clear either UK and Commonwealth rights, or world English language rights, or world rights (if your publisher is hoping to sell foreign language editions of your work). Your publisher may expect you to be solely responsible for obtaining permissions, but this job can be split between the author and the publisher – this is definitely something that you should discuss in advance, especially if you know that you are likely to be quoting significantly from other sources.

Sometimes, if the suggested quotation is over 200 words long, or if illustrated material is involved, a hefty permission fee will be demanded from whoever owns copyright and you may be liable for this. For this reason it's best to keep any quotations from books still in copyright – where the author has been dead for less than seventy-five years – as short as possible, and to give full credit to the book, author and publisher in your acknowledgements or bibliographic section.

REVISIONS SCHEDULE

A most unpleasant scenario when you are an author is to submit your manuscript by the delivery date, as requested, and then wait for months while your editor gets around to reading it and getting back to you with suggestions for changes. You might like to try to avoid this hazard by asking if publishers will agree to a set a timeframe during which revisions must be sent to you.

If your book is likely to be published in subsequent revised and updated editions after the first edition has sold out, be sure the contract specifies that you will be reimbursed for any revisions that take weeks or months of your time.

CONTROL OVER TEXT

The contract should state that the publisher may not make any changes to the text, except for basic copyediting, without the express permission of the author. Your contract should specify an approximate length for the finished manuscript; if you know that your book will definitely need some illustrations or a picture section, or you want the publisher to clear permissions on your behalf, this specification should be included in the contract. (Some contracts also give an indication of the approximate price at which they plan to publish the book, though this may well be subject to change.)

CONTROL OVER TITLE

The very idea that you conceived this book, organised the information, poured your soul into expressing your ideas, slaved away on it for months – and that some newcomer then can sweep away your precious title and plunk on a different one whether you like it or not – is one of the more appalling liberties publishers are prone to take.

Fight for a contract in which the title 'is subject to mutual agreement' between the publisher and the author.

If you have a good working relationship with your editor, you will probably discuss the title and/or subtitle at some length and arrive at one you both like. Usually, if the publisher suggests a different title from your working title, it is with good reason. You will see the validity of the change and will end up loving it.

JACKET/COVER DESIGN

The design of the hardcover jacket or paperback cover is one of the areas where many authors encounter major frustrations. But I've personally never known of a contract negotiation which enabled an author to retain any control over the cover design. Maybe it happens if the book is heavily illustrated, of considerable artistic merit and the author is the artist. But, in general, publishers have lots of precedence for retaining this right, and they won't give it up.

The most you can fight for here is the right to be consulted over jacket/cover design – which doesn't mean that the publisher will take any notice of any of your suggestions.

I will discuss what you *can* do to influence the design in Step 14.

PUBLICATION SCHEDULE

Your contract should require the publisher to publish your book within, ideally, twelve, or at the most eighteen, months after your manuscript is delivered to and accepted by the publisher.

AUTHOR COPIES

The publisher will agree to provide you with a number of books free of charge for your own use. This number can be as low as five and as high as twenty, depending on whether the book is to be published in hardcover or paperback and on the size of the print run.

Author copies are intended for you to give to your nearest and dearest, along with any people who have helped you on the book. If you have received significant help from a number of people, ask the publisher if you can have more gratis author copies so no one is left out. Usually, they will happily oblige. If your book has been endorsed, or has been contributed to by people who are not actually co-authors, your contract should state that the publisher will provide them with free copies of the book as a thank-you.

It is true that your publisher's publicity department will make additional free copies available to you for promotional purposes, if they are convinced that your giveaways will be productive. But I have seen situations in which the publisher did not co-operate with the author's promotional plans, however good they were. Extra free books just weren't in the publisher's budget, and once that budget is set, publishers can be like the Rock of Gibraltar.

So negotiate up front for as many author copies as you possibly can. When you receive them, use them judiciously. And if you know that you will need extra copies, perhaps for a book launch party, or to give to reviewers or other influential contacts who might be able to generate extra sales for you, make sure that you have the option to buy further copies at a discount of at least 35 per cent.

Publishers will not want you to purchase copies of your book specifically for resale unless you have come to some arrangement with them first. However, they will usually be pleased to supply you with books on a sale or return basis if you are involved with an event – a workshop or conference, for example – at which you will have a book-selling opportunity.

INDEX

If your book is to have an index, the publisher will want to have it done by a professional but will most likely want you to pay for it. This is often non-negotiable. It really is best for a professional indexer to work on the book; creating your own index is much more difficult than it at first seems. Authors sometimes try to interpret their work while they are indexing. For example, the author may see a subject treated on a certain page, but the reader will look and not see it there.

You could ask for the cost of preparing the index to be shared with the publisher. Indexes can actually be assembled relatively cheaply, your publisher will recommend someone reliable and the Society of Indexers will tell you what rate of pay is acceptable (at the time of writing, £13 per hour).

INSURANCE

People do get sued. It happens. So make sure your contract specifies that you are covered under your publisher's liability insurance in case the two of you become the object of someone's wrath.

If your book is likely to be contentious in any way – if, for example, it is the biography of a celebrity or well-known figure and you have uncovered previously unknown facts about that figure – the publishers will need to obtain a libel report on the content from a solicitor who has experience in book publishing. The publishers may be prepared to pay for this report themselves, but often the cost (which can be considerable) is shared between the author and publisher, and sometimes it is charged to the author. If you suspect that your book will need to be read for libel, make sure that the responsibility for any charges incurred is agreed in advance.

ADVERTISEMENTS

Sometimes publishers like to advertise other books that might interest the reader and will want to place such advertisements at the back of your book. If you aren't happy about this, be sure you retain the right to approve of any such ads.

COMPETING TITLES

You will have to agree not to publish with another publishing house a book which contains substantially the same material – which is, in effect, an abridged or expanded version – as the book covered by this particular contract.

OPTION

The publisher will seek to retain the right to consider your next book project before any other publisher has the chance to see it. If you have been happy with this publisher, this isn't a problem. If you are unhappy with them, you can only hope that they don't offer you very much for your next manuscript and thus leave you free to shop around. It's perfectly reasonable for you to insist that the option should be limited to a single book and that the terms they offer must be mutually agreeable, meaning you are able to reject them if that is what you prefer to do.

Be sure the contract stipulates a reasonable time – say, six weeks after delivery of a manuscript or proposal – after which, if the publisher has not made you an offer, you can look for another publisher. And if your contract states that your publisher has the right to match or outbid any offer on your next book from another publisher, insist that this clause is removed.

TERMINATION OF AGREEMENT

If, for any reason, the publishers decide to terminate the agreement, your contract must state that rights will revert to the author, and that the publisher cannot claim a refund on any monies already paid over to the author (most likely to be in the form of the advance due on signature, or of any expenses incurred).

A NOTE ABOUT THE SEQUENCE OF EVENTS

If you are reading this book in portions, only as you need each one, you need to know that, while the next five Steps, 12 to 16, are in the approximate order they will occur in your life, I encourage you to read them all at once. You may need to pay attention to some production and promotion concerns before you have actually completed the writing and revising of your manuscript.

Write Your Book
(If You Haven't Already)

Time required: Six months minimum.

If you wrote your manuscript before you sold it, you can *(get to work)* skip this step now. But, if you sold your book on the *(get to work)* basis of a proposal only, now is *(get to work)* when your fun begins.

Refer to *(get to work)* my suggestions in Step 6 *(get to work)* for encouragement and ideas about *(get to work)* how to write.

I've been studying the science of subliminal messages *(get to work)* and have embedded some in this chapter. I hope *(get to work)* you find them useful.

Get to work!

Deliver and Then Revise Your Manuscript

Time required: 50 to 150 hours over a period of one to four months.

If all goes according to plan, you will triumphantly mail your completed manuscript by special delivery on the day before the 'delivery date' in your contract, so that on the day itself, your editor will receive your opus. Then, a friend or loved one will take you out for a leisurely dinner and night on the town. (If no one offers, ask! Take care of yourself. Create some kind of a celebration. You deserve it!)

Of course, variations on perfection do frequently occur. For one thing, your contract may have included an earlier delivery date by which you were required to submit some portion of the manuscript, for example the first three chapters. Or you may be working with an editor who likes to see chapters as you write them, and you have been working with her suggestions all along.

Sometimes, people actually complete their work ahead of the due date. (Rare, but I hear that once upon a time, it did happen.)

Or maybe you aren't quite ready on your due date. This is a bit less rare. If you are almost ready, but you require a few more weeks, turn in what you do have complete and tell your editor the rest will be along shortly.

However, if something unforeseen occurs in your life that will delay your work by months, you need to be in touch with your editor as soon as you can see that you will be late. Tell your agent, and either she or you will request an extension of the deadline in writing, and receive back an addendum to your contract that gives you the extra time you need.

Stay in touch with your agent and editor as your writing progresses. If you have never written a book, it is very hard to estimate how long it will take you to write one. No one expects you to be superhuman. As soon as you realise you might not make your deadline, talk to your agent. Avoid the common syndrome of being in denial about time, or telling yourself that next month will be different and you'll make up for lost time – and then springing your inability to deliver on the publisher at the last minute.

One way or the other, you deliver your manuscript.

Here's a little clue that you may find invaluable later on: In the cover letter when you return the manuscript, after your 'Here it is! Hope you like it!' or whatever, say something like this to your editor: 'When you edit, I'd appreciate it very much if you could say a word or two about why you have suggested the change, if it isn't obvious. Thanks!' (More about this later.)

Now you have at least three to six weeks off while your editor edits. Catch up on your unread e-mails, call the friends you've been neglecting, tackle your huge in-tray, but above all, spend extra time with your family to make up for the stress you have all been through while you carved out the extra time you needed to write.

One day, before you know it, you will receive the manuscript back with comments written all over it. Your editor may also include a report discussing major problems she has identified or any significant overall changes she wants to suggest. She may also phone to discuss these.

Be open to your editor's suggestions. Try to strike a balance between standing up for what is truly important to you and being flexible and easy to work with. If your editor wants to suggest a major modification that is non-negotiable for you and you arrive at an impasse, remember that you are paying for an experienced advocate, your agent. Don't hesitate to enlist her support.

The editor of my first book, *If I'm So Wonderful, Why Am I Still Single?*, felt strongly that I should address the book to women, on the theory that only women read such books. Her suggestion flew in the face of everything I stood for. I believed the publishing industry was perpetuating an increasingly obsolete stereotype about men by systematically excluding them from self-help literature, and that if we ever hope to end the gender gap, we have to stop polarising and work together. Besides, I knew men responded positively to my work since they had been attending my workshops in droves.

My agent and I made a strong case; my editor caved in, and even later agreed that we were right.

Just as often, of course, editors make suggestions that greatly strengthen a book's message, organisation or marketability. Part of the reason you have entered into partnership with seasoned experts is to take advantage of their wisdom and experience. Again with my first book, my editor told me I needed a great many more anecdotes than I had included. At first I rebelled and told her I didn't want to fill the book with 'fluff'. But she insisted, and as I began to add stories to illustrate my points, I saw clearly how much they added to the clarity and accessibility of my precious points.

Now you will sit down and begin to revise.

Time away from your writing is an important step in the creative process. As you come back to your work fresh, after a break, you will see changes that you want to make yourself, as well as the ones your editor has suggested. At this phase, the changes might be fairly major. You may want to delete an entire subplot, change the order of events, rename a character, or even change the ending of your novel. In a non-fiction book, you may decide to combine two chapters into one, move the position of a chapter or split one chapter into two. You may want to delete large sections that seem repetitive or superfluous. There will be numerous rephrasings. You may want to add anecdotes or even make whole new points. The organisation of your material may crystallise now as it never did before.

Sometimes you will love an editor's suggestion and wonder why you didn't see this change yourself; it clearly improves the book. Inevitably however, your editor will make some suggestions that annoy you. You definitely don't have to do everything the editor suggests. The question is, how do you decide which suggestions to follow and which to disregard? Here are a few guidelines:

First, if your request for explanations of edits was successful, you will have a much easier time. I have worked with editors who scribbled all over my text with no comment as to why, and others who made little notes like, 'Repetitive. See p. 197' or 'Story goes better with second point'. These notes make a staggering difference in helping you to evaluate your editor's intentions. They spare you untold frustration and even time (it takes time to get frustrated!).

Whether or not you get helpful 'whys' from your editor, if you are in doubt, try the suggested change and see whether you like it. I have often found that changes I resisted at first turned out to be excellent.

Keep a list of the changes you decide not to make, noting the page number of each one. When you first note an item, also scribble a few notes about your reasons for not wanting to make the change, as though you will have to defend your decision to your editor (though you won't necessarily have to do this). Sometimes, just in making these notes, you will talk yourself out of your own position.

When you have worked your way through all the editorial changes suggested in the manuscript, go back and review everything on the list to see whether you still agree that you should not make the change. You will find that some problems resolve themselves because of the surrounding changes you have made. Or the requested changes will allow you to see that a point you thought you had made earlier hadn't come across.

If you like, take your manuscript and your list to your agent or to an editor whose work you respect and get a second opinion on each item. I did this when I was revising my first book and found that about half of the time, my consultant agreed with my editor and explained why, which was a great education for me, and about half the time, she agreed with me. I recommend this for the first book you revise; I learned a great deal from it.

If you are left with any fairly major disagreements with your editor, discuss them with her. Usually, you will be able to come to a compromise.

Finally, you will print out a completely revised version of your book, all tightened and polished, and once again, triumphantly entrust it to the Royal Mail. Another chance to celebrate!

Sometimes, a second round of editing will occur. If so, be grateful. It means your editor will be satisfied with nothing less than a superb book. Also, every edit helps you acquire better writing skills.

Rumours have it that quality editing is being downsized out of existence. The poor writing in some books that make it to bookshops attests to this. But quality editing is thriving in some corners of the industry. Be sure yours is one of them. If you feel your manuscript was in the hands of an amateur, or that it received a cursory or half-hearted edit, be honest with your editor. Request a more professional, more thorough edit.

After all revisions have been completed to the satisfaction of both you and your editor, your manuscript will be officially 'accepted' by your publisher. Your agent may want to put in a phone call to assure that the 'on acceptance' portion of your royalty advance is being processed and on its way to you.

The next step is the 'copy-edit'.

Four to eight weeks (more or less) after you turn in your last revisions, you should receive the copy-edited manuscript. The copy editor will have made marks all over it that are directed to the designer and typesetter. For example, she'll have indicated whether a dash is what they call an 'em dash' or an 'en dash'; she'll code each heading and subheading. But she will also go over each sentence with a fine toothcomb to be certain all the grammar, syntax and punctuation is perfect. She may also make smaller suggestions about structure, plot etc. which have just occurred to her.

You now have the task of reading every page to approve of the changes the copy editor has made. Again, anything you disagree with you are allowed to change. This time, you will need to make all your changes on the manuscript itself, not on your computer. If you want something to remain as it was, write 'stet'. That means the copy editor's change will not be made.

Theoretically, you may continue to make alterations yourself at this stage also, even major ones. This is not encouraged because it can mean copy-editing some portions of the book again, but if you see an improvement you just didn't see until now, don't hesitate to make it. You want your book to be the best it can be. If you are contemplating a major change at this stage, discuss it with your editor first.

You will need to make all your changes on the copy-edited hard copy. Your publisher will send you instructions for making changes in the copy-edited manuscript if you request them.

For my last book, I used twenty-seven hours over a period of ten days to go over my copy-edited manuscript, and I made some fairly major modifications including moving one chapter. A copy-edit approval could be completed in much less time. But don't rush. This is your last chance to make significant alterations.

Finish it and post it back. Always use a special delivery service as it would be a disaster to lose these precious marked-up pages.

Now, you face another challenge: to stop.

Trust me, a week after you return the copy-edit, you will hear an example that would perfectly illustrate a point in the book. Or you'll realise a subpoint you could have made.

Start a file for your next book, or the next edition of this one, and put the thought aside. Your readers will never know you thought of another little point or illustration. The book is done! Let yourself think about how beautifully it came out and how excited others will be to read it. Relax and enjoy your accomplishment.

Keep Your Eye on Production and Marketing Details

Time required: Fifteen minutes here,
an hour or two there over the next nine months.

Nine months is the usual gestation period for a book, from the time you deliver the revised manuscript to the publication date. It doesn't take nine months to print a book. But the whole process of editing, designing and manufacturing the book, introducing it to sales reps and presenting it in a catalogue so that booksellers will be eager to order it – in short producing, marketing and distributing the book – does generally require nine months.

Your publisher may decide upon a longer or sometimes shorter gestation period in order to bring your book out at the most strategic possible moment, a moment that is determined by a combination of factors such as when the public tends to buy this type of book, when related books will appear in bookshops, what is going on in the country in general (for example, one of my book launches was delayed so I wouldn't be trying to book TV interviews during a presidential campaign), and what other priorities the publisher has.

Publishers do not think of one book at a time; they make all their plans for groups of books, which they call 'lists' or 'seasons'. A publisher will usually have two or three lists per year, an autumn list and a spring list, or perhaps autumn, winter and spring. They will always be fitting the schedule for your book into the schedule they are planning for their entire season. All their plans for jacket designs, catalogue copy, sales sheets, marketing budgets and so on are laid out in a tentative form for their entire list. Your book is one title in this process.

To carry your book through its nine or more months of production and promotion planning, your publisher will generate various schedules that tell key people in all the different departments when the manuscript is expected from the author; when bound proofs, catalogue copy and flap copy are due; what production dates need to be met to keep the book on schedule; and dozens of other specific dates critical in the developing life of your book. These schedules act like a conveyor belt for your book.

If you are curious about it, you might ask your editor for a copy of your book's production schedule, though it contains a lot of detail that doesn't concern you, and the specific dates change often. Your editor will inform you of the production and marketing dates that are important for you.

During your nine-month wait, you can have considerable influence over your book's ultimate success by participating in several aspects of the book's production as much as you are able.

Sometimes, your ability to participate as fully as you want to may involve delicate negotiations and tact on your part. Traditionally, publishers want your participation, but only in a limited fashion. A fundamental belief of the publishing industry is that they know what is best for all books and that most authors are too inexperienced and biased to be of use. Authors are concerned only about their own books, whereas publishers have many priorities. Authors don't see the big picture. They don't know what has failed in the past. They know nothing about what sells books and why books fail in the marketplace.

When you gently ask to participate in various aspects of your book's production, be aware of the biases you are up against, and try to have some empathy for the publisher's position. Realise that your editor's last author may have been inappropriately demanding or invasive, that he or she is extremely busy with many books, that publishers believe they can do a better job without you, and that the marketing budgets for each specific title are finite.

Of course, as with most polarisations, the truth lies somewhere in the middle. Authors do need to honour the experience and the other priorities of publishers. Some of their concerns are quite separate from yours. They have to watch over many books and balance and weigh many factors.

But publishers also need to respect the needs and the contributions of authors far more than they sometimes do. Authors are much more experienced and knowledgeable in their own fields than publishers are, and authors have a right to know that their opinions, tastes, values and knowledge will not be completely disregarded. Publishers need to realise that authors cannot wholeheartedly promote their books when they are crushed or disgusted by their cover design, or they have to apologise for their titles. The author conceived the whole idea for the book and spent months and months writing it. It is appropriate for him or her to be invested in the rest of the book's process.

So, with tact and diplomacy, assert yourself. Most of the publishing disaster stories I've heard have the theme, 'I knew better at the time, but I didn't fight hard enough.' If you know deep inside, without ambivalence, that you are right, persuade your agent of the urgency of your position and fight relentlessly for your point of view.

THE SEQUENCE OF EVENTS

Let me say a word, again, about the timing of the production and marketing details I am about to discuss, as well as Steps 15 (endorsement statements) and 16 (promotion planning): *You may need to pay attention to some of these tasks before you complete your manuscript.* Your title, jacket design, basic promotion plan and some marketing decisions may occur before you complete your writing. Be sure to read Steps 14, 15 and 16 early; don't wait until you complete your writing. Then, if necessary, set your writing aside for a day or two to give attention to some marketing or production issue that demands your attention. But in general, the nine-month production period is the time for you to give major attention to Steps 14, 15 and 16.

YOUR EDITOR'S ASSISTANT

Your editor's assistant will manage many of your book's production and marketing details, so you are likely to become very good friends with him or her. During some critical weeks, I found I was on the phone to my editor's assistant every day and even several times a day. These assistants tend to be well-organised, cheerful, incredibly knowledgeable and somewhat more accessible than your editor herself, who spends much of her time in meetings or having lunch with your agent to discuss your next book. So make friends with your editor's assistant early on, and thank her often for all she is doing.

Often when I say 'editor' in the sections below, I mean 'or editor's assistant', but I haven't said so every time.

TITLE AND SUBTITLE

If you and your editor haven't already settled on the final title and subtitle for your book, decide now. Maybe the publishers changed the title when they first bought your book, but you still feel unhappy with it. Go back to the negotiating table. If at all possible, you should adore your title. Be sure it makes a positive impact on people when you randomly test it. Be sure it conveys what your book is about.

If you aren't thrilled with your title, work on it some more. If you love your old title but your publisher doesn't, and you are not happy with their alternative, do you understand their objection? Try to come up with a third title that you both like.

I learned the hard way that it is a mistake to ignore your deepest inner messages.

My second book, a study of couples whose marriages were happy and stable, got dubbed 'Now That I'm Married, Why Isn't Everything Perfect?' early on. Deep in my gut, I never liked this title. My book was not going to answer that question; it wasn't one more book about marital *problems*, it was about the exact opposite: what thriving couples have in common. I wanted to call it 'Couples Who Thrive', or something along those lines.

I felt this strongly. But I was thrown off by delightful public reaction to the title. It followed so nicely on from the title of my first book, *If I'm So Wonderful, Why Am I Still Single?*, that people always chuckled when they heard it. I failed to listen to my intuition.

Then I found myself on my promotional tour, having to answer journalists and TV and radio presenters who asked, 'Why does your book have such a negative title? It is such a positive book.' It was heartbreaking.

The epilogue to the story is that, two years later, everyone realised the title was a mistake, and the publisher brought out a trade paperback version of the book with a new title: *Eight Essential Traits of Couples Who Thrive*.

Your title is so important. Don't compromise.

JACKET OR COVER DESIGN

Here's how jackets get designed:

Your editor gives her design department or a freelance designer a synopsis of your book and a design brief. (Designers rarely read the whole book.) The designers respond with several designs. When your editor and the marketing and publicity people settle on the one they like, they will send you a copy. If all goes well, you will be thrilled with the design. Perhaps you will have a few changes you would like to suggest – in the copy, the colours or the ideas. Convey these to your editor. Either they will make the changes, or they will try to persuade you that your idea won't work best in the long run.

When you first receive your preliminary jacket design, whether you love it, hate it, or are somewhere in between, live with it for a few days before you react. Show it around. Are you getting mixed reactions? Or universally positive or negative ones?

If you are unsure whether you like your jacket design or not, or if you are pretty sure you don't, show it to a few independent booksellers. They are the closest to what sells and what doesn't, and their opinions are often useful. Listen to them. Maybe they will persuade you that your jacket isn't so bad.

However, if after several days, you and several booksellers agree the jacket has a major drawback, write to your editor. Mention what you *do* like about the cover first. Then, be very specific about what you don't like and why. Name the booksellers you spoke to and quote them exactly; their opinions may carry more weight than your own by itself.

Unfortunately, sometimes what you will receive in return is a defence of the design the publishers have already decided upon.

Why do publishers insist on covers authors don't like?

They claim to possess secret, inside information, unavailable to the rest of us, about what types of designs make books sell, as though we can't all go to bookshops and study the jacket designs of bestselling books, and as though all bestselling jacket designs actually have something in common. Or they may say we lay people don't understand the principles of design. In addition, the publishers' goals are sometimes different from the author's. Whereas you want the design to be readable and attractive, the publisher may be trying to achieve a certain 'look' for a line of books.

I have witnessed jacket disputes in which the author and agent did everything but stage a hunger strike in the publishers' office, but the publishers still went ahead with their first design. Look in a bookshop: You will see jackets that are virtually unreadable, messy or ugly, next to jackets that almost leap off the shelf with their message. Are publishers' designers the repository of the only known wisdom on the subject of jacket designs? I'm one who doubts it.

Designers *can* come up with new jacket designs if they choose to, and quickly too. In one case, an author had been shown a beautiful, bold simple cover she loved. At the last minute, the buyer for one of the big bookchains said he wouldn't buy any books unless the subtitle appeared on the cover. In a week, the design department produced an entirely different jacket – new colours and new concept. (If the first one was a 'bestselling design', how could the second one be also? They were different in every way.)

To help ensure that you are not among the (relatively few) authors who have to live with book jackets they don't love, I strongly encourage you to follow a preventative strategy and take the initiative ahead of time.

TAKE THE INITIATIVE EARLY

What can you do before you receive your jacket design to maximise the chances that you will love it? Here are a few different possibilities:

1. Find an artist or graphic designer whose work you love, and design your own jacket. Publishers do not encourage this, and if you ask first, you will probably be told it is against company policy. So don't ask; just show up with a design. You run the risk of paying a considerable amount for a design they reject. In fact, it is rare for a publisher to accept an author's design, but I do know of one author whose design was accepted. It was done by a professional designer who had designed book jackets before.

    You will need to present your cover design early so the editor receives it before the design department has gone to work on their own version.

2. A less expensive alternative with a higher probability of success, and one I highly recommend, is to send your editor a detailed memo with your ideas about the jacket design. Again, do this early,

within a month or two after you first sell your book. Or ask your editor when design discussions on your book will begin to take place and send your memo before then. The timing doesn't coincide with your book's production schedule so much as with the schedule for a whole 'season' of books.

First, visit a bookshop and study jackets, especially, but not exclusively, in your book's section of the bookshop. If you have a designer friend you trust, bring him or her along. Find jackets you like; what do they have in common? Find jackets you don't like; why don't they work? What colours are you drawn to? Are there typefaces you like or don't like? Do you like covers that incorporate a photograph or drawing? Is there a design style (like Old English or post-modern) that you feel would be appropriate for your book?

What are your top criteria for a book jacket? For example, you may envision a cover that is pretty, bold, sexy, classy, feminine or masculine, funny, zany, dignified, bright, striking or soft. You may feel strongly that your jacket must be easy to read, innovative and distinctive or uncluttered. You may even want to become more specific and suggest bold letters, contrast between the background colour and the letters themselves, or a specific style of type. Is there a particular illustration, photograph or painting that you think would be perfect on the cover of your book?

Consider including colour photocopies of a few jackets that illustrate points you are trying to make to your editor, or jackets you especially like or do not like, and explain why.

If you have some elements or qualities that you either must have or cannot tolerate, say so. But otherwise, phrase your desires as requests, not demands, and say something about not wanting to unduly restrict the creativity of the designers. Say everything that is truly important to you, but also remember, the fewer suggestions you make, the easier it will be for the designer to address your most important concerns.

Of course, send a copy of everything to your agent.

If you don't hear from your editor, call him in a week or so to be sure he received your materials and has not buried them on his desk. Solicit his reaction. If he is appreciative and in accord with what you have written, good. Now just make sure that he will pass your memo along to the designer.

If he is unco-operative – annoyed that you have interfered in this area, or in disagreement with your opinions – alert your agent, who might be able to elicit a more co-operative response. If your editor is on your side, your chances of ending up with a cover you like are increased greatly.

3. As you approach your manuscript delivery date, ask your editor when the jacket design might be ready. Then around that time, if he hasn't sent it to you, gently enquire. Just be sure he isn't leaving you out of the loop – especially if your contract reads that you must be consulted regarding jacket design.

I hope you are in the fortunate position of being presented with a jacket design you can strongly support. Maximise your chances by sending a memo first, and then cross your fingers.

BOOK DESIGN

A book designer will be assigned to design the interior of your book, everything from the typeface that will be used to the arrangement of titles and subtitles, to spacing and graphic design elements.

If you have any special preferences about your book design, or you have seen design elements in other books that you believe would or would not be effective in yours, send a book design memo to your editor specifying exactly what you would or would not like to see in the design of your book.

If you don't have any special design requests, don't feel that you have to manufacture any. The vast majority of book designs are quite acceptable.

However, even if you make no specific suggestions, do request that your editor send you sample design pages as soon as they are available. That way, if the designer has used a design element that you find inappropriate, or you feel the design is too messy, or there is something about it that upsets you, there will be time for you to request design changes.

Probably, you won't want to make any waves about the book design. But give yourself the opportunity to see it in the form of sample design pages, just to be sure. If you don't request sample design pages, you probably won't ever see any.

In case you do not see design samples ahead of time, you can still make small changes in design when you review your page proofs.

AUTHOR QUESTIONNAIRE

At some point, probably while you are still writing your manuscript, your publisher's publicity department will ask you to complete a lengthy questionnaire. They will ask about your background, your credentials, cities where you have lived or worked, your publishing history – everything that might provide ammunition for them as they plan their publicity for your book.

Provide them with as much information as you can. Show them you are imaginative, thorough and eager to co-operate.

CATALOGUE COPY

Each publishing season, your publisher will prepare a catalogue of their forthcoming books from which booksellers can order. At some point, your editor should show you the catalogue copy she or the promotion department has written about your book. (If she doesn't, ask to see it.)

Editors and marketing directors tend to be fairly skilled at writing these catalogue descriptions, I've found. Your editor will have completed a thorough reading of as much of your manuscript as is available at the time the catalogue copy must be written, and she will know what she liked and why.

Nevertheless, after you see the copy, you may have suggestions for improvement. Give all your feedback to your editor. If you feel the publisher did a great job with the copy, don't forget to be complimentary and appreciative.

If you have been promoting your work in brochures or newsletters, if you have ever had promotional material on your book topic written by a professional copywriter, or if you have strong ideas about what should be emphasised in the catalogue copy, you may want to send a 'catalogue-copy memo' to your editor, just as you did for the jacket design. Catalogue copy is important, but not nearly as critical as the jacket and the title of your book.

SALES CONFERENCE

Sales reps for your publisher are stationed all over the country, busily visiting independent booksellers, national bookshop chains and wholesalers, and convincing them to stock your book – along with several hundred others that they also represent.

Several times each year, the publisher brings them all together for a sales conference. The publisher presents all their forthcoming books with as much fanfare and enthusiasm as possible to get the sales reps excited about representing these books to booksellers.

Your editor may ask you for photographs, or special display material, or for audio or video footage of yourself giving a presentation or appearing on TV or radio. Supply her with whatever you have. If your publisher believes that you are sufficiently interesting and entertaining (and it is your job to convince her of this), she may even invite you to attend the sales conference in person, to give a short presentation of your forthcoming book.

Seize this opportunity with both hands. Make your presentation as lively and memorable as possible, so it stands out from the numerous other presentations that the reps have had to endure during the conference. Where appropriate – for a cookery book, for example – bring samples of your wares for the reps to try. Exploit the timing of your presentation if you can: if it takes place just before lunch, serve all the reps with an aperitif – that will impress them and make them remember your name. Use whatever props, visual or audio aids are at your disposal to bring life and colour to your words.

With my last book, my editor invited me to write a short statement directly to the sales reps and then go into a local sound studio and record it. My short rap about the brilliance of my book and my plans for promotion was to be put on an audio tape with similar pep talks from other authors, so the reps could listen to it in their cars as they travelled to and from appointments. If your publisher isn't creating such a tape for its reps, suggest the idea to your editor.

Bear in mind that each sales rep represents hundreds of books, and that, as much as they might like to, they can't maintain a relationship with each individual author. The publisher puts a lot of effort into managing the amount of mailings, phone calls, audio cassettes and so forth that sales reps receive by giving them information about groups of books, rather than one book at a time. So funnel the information you want your sales reps to receive through your editor, and trust that they are doing the best job they can for you.

FLAP COPY AND BACK COPY

You will have the opportunity to see the promotional copy that will appear on the front and back jacket flaps of your book, and also on the back cover (or on the book itself if your book is a paperback). Review it carefully when you receive it. Does the copy convey what you feel is most enticing about your book? If you didn't know anything about this book, would these words convince you to buy it?

If you know what you want your book jacket to say and you have good promotional writing skills, you may want to write up some flap copy and back jacket copy very early on – maybe just before you complete your manuscript – and send it to your editor as a suggestion. Especially if you have been promoting your material for years and you know what headlines and bullet points grab people's attention, send this information to your editor early and suggest it be considered by the jacket-copy writer.

Again, I have found that editors and copywriters do a wonderful job with flap copy. With my first book, I didn't like what they wrote and completely rewrote it from scratch. Then I read both versions to several people, and they all chose the one written by the professionals! I decided I liked it after all. But I have also had the experience of improving upon what I received.

AUTHOR PHOTO

A photo of you, often on the back jacket flap, or possibly the back cover of a paperback, is a nice touch for readers. They spend time getting to know you through your work; they love knowing a little more about you and seeing what you look like.

Start preparing for your author photo *early*, preferably the moment you sell your book. Women, it may take you several visits to the hairdresser to decide how you want your hair in the photo. If you are going to use a style consultant to help dress you for your promotional appearances, use her for the photo too. (More about style consultants in Step 18.)

Author photos don't have to be conservative headshots. You are allowed to have some freedom, to let the photo express something about who you are. Sit on a swing or railing. Hold your beloved dog or cat. Stand in front of your rose bush. Curl up on a sofa.

Talk to your editor before you do a shoot for your photo. It is important that the photo matches the subject matter and tone of the book, and your editor may have some suggestions. Later, when you are trying to decide which of several photos you will choose, definitely bring your editor into the discussion.

Take a roll or two of snapshots in which you try out a variety of outfits, settings, positions and maybe even hairstyles. From those, select the combinations you like most. This will save you time and money when you go for the actual shoot. If possible, treat yourself to a professional photographer, one who comes highly recommended.

PAGE PROOFS

A month or two after you give the copy-edited manuscript back to your editor, she will send you proofs, pages printed up as they will actually appear in the book. Usually, you will have just two weeks or so to read and return them. Most publishers also have the proofs read 'professionally', in-house or by a freelance proof reader. But don't rely on them.

Give yourself a lot of time to read through the page proofs very carefully. Proofread for typos and misspellings. Re-check your chapter titles. Do you like the way the book design turned out? For example, with one of my books, the subtitles were indented and I felt they would look much better flush left. The publisher complied with my request.

You may still make a few changes to the text. Most contracts allow you to make up to 10 per cent of the typesetting changes at this stage at your discretion without having to pay extra. (The other 90 per cent of the changes will be to correct typos or make changes that were the typesetter's errors.) So take out a sentence or change a word here and there if you like. This really *is* your last chance to polish. But also remember that heavy changes at this stage will mean delays and additional expense – and annoyance for the publisher.

ACCESS INFORMATION

As a courtesy to your readers, in case they want to write to tell you how your incredible book changed their lives, consider putting your mailing address and e-mail address at the end of the book. (This is usually only appropriate in the case of non-fiction books.) You will definitely want to do this if you offer workshops or lectures, or if you have other products available such as audio or video tapes.

FIRST SERIAL, FOREIGN AND BOOK CLUB RIGHTS

As soon as your manuscript is ready, your agent or publisher (whoever retained these rights in the contract) can start sending it to magazines in an attempt to sell first serial rights, and to foreign agents in an attempt to sell your book to foreign publishers. To be sure, some books are more conducive to serialisation and to book club and foreign sales than others. But, when your manuscript is complete, ask your agent what is happening on these fronts.

If you have a relaxed Type I agent who gives you the equivalent of a blank stare over the phone, and if you know of magazines that could be quite interested in an excerpt from your book, or you believe foreign readers would be interested in your material, you don't have to take no for an answer. Tell your agent you would like her to manage these matters for you.

There are subagents who manage foreign sales for agents who are not equipped to do so themselves. Encourage your agent to use one of these people if she seems disinclined to do it herself.

It is unlikely that your publishers would ask to buy first serial, book club and foreign rights if they had no intention of exercising them, so if your publisher has these rights, you probably don't need to worry. But ask anyway. Let your editor know that you are eager to be kept up to date on these sales.

SUMMARY

The production and promotion planning phases of your book are the ones in which your relationship with your editor and others at your publishing house are the most delicate – and the most critical. For best results, I recommend these general strategies:

1. Make yourself likeable and easy to work with. No matter how unhappy or angry you are about something, or how powerless you feel, a spirit of goodwill is likely to bring you better results than an angry, self-righteous tirade.
2. Take the initiative, and take it early. Submit all your suggestions, hopes and desires to your editor early, in writing, and with the greatest of respect. Don't back anyone into a corner with non-negotiable demands.
3. Choose the items that matter the most to you, and concentrate on

them. The fewer earnest requests you make, the more likely you are to have them taken into consideration.

4. Don't forget about your agent. If you encounter a difficult negotiation with your editor or publicist, consider asking your agent to intervene for you. Your agent has more clout than you do, because your publisher needs that relationship in the future. Also, your agent may have better negotiating skills than you.

5. If you wish the publishing world were set up differently and that authors had more power, consider joining the Society of Authors or the Writers' Guild. Not only will they be able to advise you on good practice within the publishing industry, they will also take up cudgels on your behalf if you have any serious complaints against your publisher.

Solicit Endorsements

*Time required: Two full days plus five or six partial days
over a period of three months.*

Endorsements sell books. If you can get God to say, 'This is the best
book on _____ that has ever been written,' readers
are bound to be curious. You have probably purchased a book on
impulse yourself because someone you admire raved about it on the
cover.

As soon as you submit your completed manuscript for the first
time, while you are waiting for the editor's comments to begin your
revisions, begin the process of obtaining endorsements. Here's how:

1. DISCUSS ENDORSEMENTS WITH YOUR EDITOR

Editors often seek endorsements for the books they oversee, but some
editors are more aggressive about it than others. Make it clear to your
editor that you are eager to help with this task. Stay in close touch
with her, and divide up the work, as I'll suggest below, but take the
initiative. Don't leave the whole thing up to her.

Editors sometimes wait until the page proofs for your book are
ready, and then send them to a few authors they know or believe would
be good endorsers for you. If you wait for this, you will be waiting too
long. Sometimes the time between the proofs and the completed jacket
(where you want the blurbs to appear) is only a few weeks. You are
asking busy people to read a whole book for you. Give them plenty of
time by sending your manuscript early. Don't wait for page proofs.

2. MAKE A WISH LIST

List everybody you can think of whose positive comments about your
book would be meaningful. If the person has an impressive title, he or
she does not need to be a famous author or a celebrity. For example,
if you are writing a history of the Confederation of British Industries,

current or former Director Generals of the CBI would be impressive endorsors.

Don't shy away from famous people. Never leave a name off the list because you think, 'I'll never get that person!' Thinking small will never get you beyond small time. Think of experts on your topic; other authors in your field; TV, radio and movie celebrities who have something to do with your field; relevant political figures; or anyone else with a well-known name or title whose opinion on your work would be significant.

Consult both your editor and your agent. Both of them will have suggestions for your list and may have connections you lack.

3. RELIST THE NAMES IN ORDER OF PRIORITY

Start by making two priority lists. On the first, list the endorsements you would most like to obtain, your wish list. On the second, list the names in the order in which you guess you are most likely to succeed in persuading the person to endorse your book.

Now, matching up those two factors and working together with your editor, decide upon five to ten people you want to pursue.

You can start with an even larger group, of course. In general, it is more powerful to have three quality endorsements than twelve statements by people that most of us never even heard of. But you may have to start with a list of fifteen to end up with actual endorsements from three or so people.

4. SEND A PRELIMINARY LETTER INCLUDING A BRIEF SYNOPSIS OF YOUR BOOK AND A SHORT BIOGRAPHY

Decide which people on the list you will approach and which your editor will approach. She will use her connections, and you will use yours. If neither of you knows the person in question, the first letter should probably come from you. Letters from editors are more routine and easier to dismiss.

The Letter.   Here's a basic formula for a preliminary endorsement-request letter. Don't write the same letter to each person; make your letters personal.

1. Mention your personal connection, whatever it is: I heard you speak at the convention, I read your last book, we met briefly

at Tom's party, our mutual friend Susie Jones encouraged me to write, I have admired your work ever since blah-blah – or whatever. Include a complimentary or flattering comment as you make this connection. For example, your comment about xyz made a big impact on me, or I especially loved your chapter on _____, or Susie says you have been so helpful to her.

2. Say why you are writing, and exactly why you believe an endorsement from this person would be relevant and useful. Give the name of your book, the publisher and the date of publication.
3. If you have already received some endorsements, by all means mention them, especially if they are by impressive individuals.
4. Ask whether the person would be interested in seeing either the manuscript or the page proofs.
5. Thank the person for considering your request.

Here are several such letters I wrote for my third book (modified for privacy):

Dear Person-I-Know-Slightly-Through-an-Organisation:

As a fellow member of the XYZ Association and a great admirer of your work with young people as well as your wonderful book, I'd like to prevail upon your well-known generosity.

Would you consider making an endorsement statement for my forthcoming book?

Entitled *How One of You Can Bring the Two of You Together*, it will be published in February 1997 by Broadway Books, a division of Bantam Doubleday Dell.

I've enclosed a brief synopsis. I could either send you the manuscript now or the bound proofs mid-August.

In view of how incredibly busy you are, I will be extremely appreciative if you are able to give me this support. Please let me know if you would like to see any form of the book.

Congratulations on all your success.

Dear Mr Person-with-whom-I-have-no-direct-connection:

You write so beautifully! I've just looked through *Book Title* again and it is a pleasure to read. It is easy to see why your books are so well received.

Because a strong theme in your work is finding ways to take good care of yourself, I thought of you as an ideal person to endorse my latest work, entitled *How One of You Can Bring the Two of You Together.* Self-love and self-nurturing figure strongly in this book as well.

I've enclosed a brief synopsis to give you an idea of the direction of my work. I would be thrilled if you would like to take a look at either a manuscript, which I could get to you immediately, or the page proofs, which are due mid-August, and consider making a statement of endorsement.

The book will be published in February 1997 by Broadway Books, a division of Bantam Doubleday Dell.

Thanks so much for taking a moment to consider my request.

Dear Person-I-Know-Somewhat:

More than a year ago, I had a brief phone conversation with you in which I asked you about your workshop entitled, 'XYZ'. Thank you so much for the very helpful information you gave me at that time. I have also found *Book Title* to be a wonderfully useful, well-organised book brimming with great information and stories.

I have now completed my own book (my third) in which I isolate the idea that one person working alone can achieve excellent results in a relationship. Entitled *How One of You Can Bring the Two of You Together,* it will be published in February 1997 by Broadway Books.

I'm writing to ask whether you would consider reviewing my manuscript and, if you like it, making a statement of endorsement. I have enclosed a brief synopsis to give you an idea of the direction of my work.

I can send you the manuscript now, or the bound page proofs will be ready mid-August if you prefer that format. Please let me know if you would like to see any form of the book.

I admire and appreciate you for all you have done to make [your work] accessible to more people. I will be extremely grateful if you are interested in reviewing my work.

The Synopsis.   With your letter, include a one- or two-page synopsis of your book and the table of contents.

To write your synopsis, consider using wording from the catalogue or flap copy, if you have seen those already, or wording from the 'sell page' of your proposal. You may want to summarise each chapter ever so briefly, or summarise groups of chapters. Keep this *brief* and try to make it so intriguing that the reader will be very curious to see more.

The Biography.   Either in your letter or on a separate page, offer some information about who you are, what your expertise on this subject is, and your writing and publishing history, if any.

You may have to be resourceful to locate addresses for some of your potential endorsers. See my suggestion in Step 9 about contacting authors through their publishers. A good reference librarian may be able to help you, and your editor will have suggestions. Some of the people on your list will probably be in your own extended professional family, and you'll be able to network your way to their addresses.

5. FOLLOW UP

When you receive a request for a manuscript, send it out promptly with a grateful cover letter. It's inexpensive to print manuscripts on your own computer printer, but each one may require an hour or so. If you decide to pay a copy shop to duplicate them, consider printing on two sides of each page and using a plastic spiral binding. It saves paper, and looks less formidable to the recipient.

Or, your publisher may be willing to send the manuscripts out for you. But if you sent the initial letter, you should probably write the cover letter yourself.

If you hear nothing for two or three weeks after you send your initial letter, phone to ask whether the person received it. Follow up by phone also if you send out a manuscript or galley and then hear nothing for a while.

Since you are starting this process early, you can check in every couple of weeks on the status of each of your requests. Keep persisting until you either succeed or are turned down by each person you approached.

6. WRITE A THANK-YOU

When you receive an endorsement, even if you have been able to speak with the person over the phone as often happens when you are discussing the actual wording, write an enthusiastic, personal thank-you note to your endorser. Sometimes your editor's assistant will send one too, but don't let that substitute for your own sincere gratitude. Authors are busy, and they are putting their reputation at stake by endorsing your work. It is a great favour. You might even want to consider sending a gift.

As soon as your book is published, be sure your editor sends each endorser a complimentary copy of it.

Author Sam Horn suggests getting in touch with your endorsers a year after your book is published to bring them up to date on sales figures, reviews, press and media attention, and the general success of the book. This is especially thoughtful and gives you yet another opportunity to thank busy authors for giving you a boost.

And don't forget, later on when another author asks *you* for an endorsement, offer your support if you possibly can.

Plan Your Own Promotion and Publicity

Time required: Varies.

YOU ARE IN CHARGE

Writing your book is only half of your job as an author.

Now, you have to do everything you can to be sure that the people who might be interested in buying it know it exists.

'But isn't that the publisher's job?' you may ask.

No. Publishers publish and distribute books. If you want to assure your book's success, you need to be its director of marketing and promotion. Your publisher will assist you. But the quality and quantity of promotion support offered by the publisher varies enormously from book to book. *It is you who must mastermind the publicity campaign for your book. Never depend on your publisher to do this,* no matter how much or how little they are planning to help. If you receive support from your publisher's publicity department, consider this a bonus.

One advantage of being your own director of marketing and promotion is that you can be innovative, something publishers are not famous for. Whereas a corporation like IBM will search out the smartest MBAs they can find to plan their marketing and will pay them huge sums of money, publishers tend to hire 22-year-olds who just graduated from university with a degree in English literature. Then they tell them, 'Here's how we do it.' This is not a problem for you, because they know how to do what they do, and they do it extremely well. But you don't need to stop with the contribution they make to promoting your book.

First-time authors often make three mistakes: (1) They don't start thinking about promoting their book until it is published (which is much too late), and then (2) all they do about promoting it is badger their publisher to 'do more'. Also, (3) they plan promotion for too short a period of time.

How can you avoid these three mistakes?

First, recognise that no matter what your publisher does or does not do, you are the director of marketing for your own book. Take charge. I'll be more specific about how in a moment.

Second, start early. As soon as you deliver your completed manuscript, go to work on your marketing and promotion plan. You have at least nine months to set yourself up. Use it well.

Third, recognise that the success of most books is determined by the first year or eighteen months of the book's life, not the first three months.

You will hear a lot about how you have to make your book succeed in the first three months, or the book is doomed. The first three months *are* critical, and here is why: Three months after your book hits the bookshops, all the publishers, including your own, will be presenting bookshops with their *next* round of fabulous, exciting, blockbuster books. Bookshops have limited shelf space, so they will clear out all the old books (your book is already old after three months) to make room for the new ones. After three months, you will be competing with even your own publisher's new books. And don't forget, publishing is the only industry in the world in which retailers can return merchandise they have already purchased for a full refund. If your book hasn't been selling well in its first three months, it will disappear from the bookshops, and after that, even an appearance on a prime time TV show will do you little good.

So it is true that you have to make a major effort in the first three months. But it is a terrible mistake to stop after that. The best promotion a book can possibly receive is word of mouth. Word of mouth takes time to build, and you have to keep nurturing it. Also, continue to do radio interviews, workshops, magazine articles, lectures – you can let booksellers know this (more about how in Step 18). Knowing you are continuing to promote heavily will encourage them to select somebody else's book to return to the publisher, not yours.

John Gray's hugely successful *Men Are from Mars, Women Are from Venus,* didn't hit the bestseller lists until nine months after it was published. After the first three months, it was selling briskly enough to be kept in the bookshops. But after that, John told me, he continued to conduct workshops all over the country, and he did five to ten radio interviews every week.

Make plans now to create a major splash with your book during its first three months of publication, and to sustain your promotion efforts at a strong level for a full year.

Paperback originals are less likely to be removed from bookshops after three months. They are generally seen as books that will endure, that will continue to sell steadily, possibly for years. (Books with this profile, including hardcovers that go into paperback after one year, are called 'backlist' books, meaning the bookshops are encouraged to keep them in stock all the time, to keep reordering them.) So with paperback originals, the initial splash is less important, and the sustained, continuing promotion activities are the secret to success.

One more reason a year-long promotion plan is critical: No matter how much your publisher assists you with your initial promotion efforts, unless your book's sales are really accelerating or publicity interest remains high, they will virtually abandon you after one to three months. They have other books to launch. Anticipate this. It's the way the whole industry is set up. If you want your book to stay in bookshops and continue to receive attention after one or two months, you will have to promote it yourself.

Your own promotion campaign will be determined by the amount of passion for success, imagination, time and money you begin with. If you have or can acquire at least two of these four essentials, your book has a good chance of succeeding. The more of them you possess, the easier and more successful your publicity campaign will be.

Here are my suggestions for how to plan your promotion. Begin as soon as possible after your manuscript is complete.

BRAINSTORM

Begin by brainstorming. By yourself or together with several friends, think up everything you might do to make the public aware of your book when it comes out. If possible, include in your brainstorm group people with a variety of expertise and experience in general selling and marketing, book promotion, copywriting or just general creativity.

Your list might look something like this:

Radio and TV interviews
Newspaper articles
Magazine articles

Newsletter reviews or articles
Book reviews
Speeches before related audiences
Fliers mailed or distributed to target groups
Direct mail campaign to a target group
Relevant associations and organisations
   buy an ad or write an article for their newsletter
   speak at their convention
   hold a booth at their convention to sell books
Workshops or lectures around the country
Author events at bookshops

The only limit to strategies is your imagination. Every book has some unique possibility. You may not be able to carry out every activity you brainstorm, but now is not the time to censor and select. Think up every outrageous scheme you can! You'll get to choose what to do later.

ESTABLISH YOUR MARKETING PLAN

When you feel satisfied that you have gathered together the best potential promotion ideas for your book, begin to group and prioritise them. What ideas seem most cost-effective? What strategies are especially appropriate for your book? Which ones would have the greatest impact where you want it? Which ones are best suited to your talents, your lifestyle and your budget?

Now make up a definite marketing plan. Being realistic about the amount of time, money and commitment you have, list the items you definitely plan to accomplish and by when, and the items you would like to accomplish if time and money permit. List assistance and resources you will require, if any. Be specific.

ASK FOR A PROMOTION MEETING

Now is the time, now that you are more knowledgeable and prepared, to talk with your publisher's promotion department.

Guess what? They have been putting together a marketing plan for your book too!

When a publisher buys your book, part of what they are buying is your interest in and ability to promote your book. That's why they will pay more if you have impressive credentials, previous media experience, a workshop series, personality and enthusiasm. They are counting on you.

The moment they buy your book, they prepare a tentative profit and loss statement in which they begin to 'position' the book in their minds. How much have we invested in this book? Is this a book that has the potential to be a big hit? Based on previous experience with books like this, do we expect it to sell 2,000 copies, 20,000 copies or 50,000 copies? How large a marketing and promotion budget should we plan for this book?

As the book begins to take shape, the original budget figures change depending on what else is happening within the publishing house, what is going on in the marketplace, how the book itself is turning out, and many other factors.

At some point, the various departments at your publishing house come together for a meeting about your book. The marketing department, the publicity department, your editor, the sales department – they are all there. Together they decide upon an overall marketing strategy for your book. Will it be driven mainly by advertising in strategic places? By media interviews? By special sales, like direct mail? What is the overall budget for this book, and how will it be divided up? They end up with a marketing plan for your book.

Would it make sense for you and your publisher to be talking together sooner since you are both planning an overall strategy?

Not really, as it turns out. You and they have widely different considerations. Your book is your number one priority. For them, it is one of many priorities. You know what zeal, money, time and talents are available to you; they know what money and whose time and energy is available to them. You have one vision for your book; they may have the same vision – or quite a different one from yours.

But the main reason it is not necessary for you to talk sooner is that, with rare exceptions, you will have very little influence on their decisions, no matter what you do or say. They have a certain amount of money and time they must divide up among a lot of books. They can't take the time to give you their big picture, but when they have made their decisions about your book, that's it. About the only thing that will change their minds is a book that begins to perform wildly beyond their expectations. If your book takes off, you *might* be able to make a compelling case that they should give your book more of their promotional resources.

Your main opportunity to try to influence your publisher earlier is the author questionnaire (see Step 14). That is why it is important to give it careful attention. It gives your publishers concrete ideas of areas to push, places where you already have a presence they might capitalise on, and methods of marketing that are likely to work best for your book.

So, let your publisher plan and envision, while you separately plan and envision. Then, you initiate a promotion meeting.

Ask your editor whom you should speak to about your promotion plan for your book. She may want to talk with you herself. Or she may refer you to whoever in the marketing or publicity department has been assigned to your book. If no one has been assigned yet, she may refer you to the head of one of these departments. Let's say she tells you to speak to David.

Before your promotion meeting, which may be over the phone or in person, post David a letter in which you outline your own plans for promotion and anything you would like to ask the publisher to do or to help with. Send a copy of the letter to your editor and your agent.

As the marketing director for your book, you have three goals for this meeting: (1) to find out exactly what your publisher has decided to do for your book so that you can factor this information into your overall marketing plan; (2) to ask your publisher for specific types of support; and (3) to solicit your publisher's opinion of the plan you have put together.

If your requests for support are very specific and not terribly time-consuming or expensive, there is a very good chance you can get your publisher's co-operation. For example, let's say you have decided that a flier about your book is an important component of your campaign and that you plan to distribute it at workshops and conferences. You might see whether your publisher would be willing to absorb the cost of printing it. Or one author I know decided that giving free books to line managers in large multi-level marketing organisations would be a super strategy, since she was certain they would recommend it to all the distributors in their line. She asked the publisher to provide her with the free books.

David will probably agree to provide some of the help you ask for but not all of it. If you get turned down on a request you feel is both important and reasonable, fight for your cause. Ask your agent to support your request. Stay polite and understanding, but be assertive.

Remember that facts and statistics are more persuasive than emotions.

Ask David to comment on your marketing plan. He may encourage you to proceed with strategies one to four, but tell you that strategies five and six have rarely worked in the past and are probably not worth your effort. Or he may suggest strategies that did not occur to you, or that you rejected. Take advantage of his expertise and experience.

PRINT RUN

After your promotion meeting, have a separate discussion with your editor about the approximate number of books the publishers are planning to print in the first print run. This is her area of responsibility, not the marketing or publicity department's. You want to be sure the size of the first print run your publisher is planning is commensurate with the marketing campaign you are planning.

If you are planning a massive marketing campaign, and they are printing and distributing only 3,000 books, you can't possibly sell 30,000 books. Of course they can print more, but maybe not as soon as you need them. If your publicity is wildly successful, but all the bookshops have run out of books, your grand effort will be useless.

Publishers have lots of experience determining how many books to print. Though they have been known to miscalculate badly in both directions, usually the planned print run will be appropriate. Persuading a publisher to change their print run numbers can be difficult. But if you have an extraordinary promotion and marketing campaign in place involving serious time and money, you may be able to do it.

PROMOTIONAL TOURS

Long before you get to the stage of your promotion meeting, you will probably already know whether or not your publisher is planning an author tour for you. Often, they will ask about your availability for a tour when they buy the book. Significant author tours are usually announced in the catalogue, so you may learn of your author tour – or lack thereof – when you see the copy for your catalogue page. Or just ask your editor; she will have a general idea quite early of what is being planned for your book.

You probably hope that your publisher will send you round the country and book you on lots of radio and TV shows. Sometimes, they may plan a satellite tour for you instead. That's when you sit in one room for three hours and get patched into fifteen live radio shows all over the country for five-minute segments each.

Media tours are good publicity for some books, but they are not *necessary* for success, and they are not *enough* by themselves. Whether you have an author tour or not, you have to support your book with other promotion strategies. If your publisher does give you a media tour, be sure you have carefully laid plans for continuing the momentum when your tour is over. (More about your media tour itself in Step 18.)

If you learn that little or no TV or radio publicity is planned, you may be disappointed or irate. And before you even try it, let me assure you that any pleading, ranting and raving, sobbing, shouting or badgering you do will be to no avail.

Media tours are not appropriate for all books. Some are not of wide enough appeal. Even if you think the public *ought* to be interested in your topic, or that they would be if they could only hear you, the publicist may know that it will be very hard to get you bookings. Only last month, she had to cancel a five-city tour that had been planned for an author because TV and radio producers and journalists just didn't respond to her press releases. She couldn't get the author booked.

If the publishers didn't invest very much money in your book, they may feel that they can't afford to send you on tour.

I have worked with several authors who told their publishers, 'I will pay for my own travel to several cities. Will you book the media appearances for me?' Seems like a reasonable request, but publishers often say no, and with good reason. First, setting up a media tour requires a great deal of someone's time, time that may already have been allocated for some other book. Second, maybe bookshops didn't purchase the book in large enough numbers to make a media tour useful. The publisher can't control what bookshops buy. If there are no books available to the public, a tour is a waste of time and money.

Whatever their reason, they have already made up their minds. No tour. It is okay to be disappointed, but don't let it stop you.

There are alternatives.

One is, you can plan your own tour. Many authors do this. Virtually always, the publisher will at the very least prepare a press release for you. You can either send it to producers and journalists yourself, or hire a professional publicist to do it for you. If you restrict yourself to radio interviews that can be done over the phone you will incur no travel expenses.

You might consider hiring a publicist to approach only the most important national radio or TV shows and newspapers. For a reasonable amount of money, you can have a seasoned professional who knows exactly how to approach these producers and editors working full time to get you national media attention. Your agent should be able to recommend a good publicist.

If you do launch your book with radio, TV and print interviews, whether booked by your publisher, a publicist you pay, or you, view your media as one component in a marketing plan that supports your book sales in a variety of ways.

I will discuss what to do while you are on your media tour in Step 18. Here, we are discussing only the *planning* of a possible tour.

WHAT ELSE MIGHT YOUR PUBLISHER DO FOR YOUR BOOK?

Though media tours sound flashy, publishers often support books in many other important ways as well.

They distribute bound page proofs for potential endorsements and review. For some books, reviews are especially important. They may print an excerpt as a small giveaway booklet to drum up interest. They sell book excerpts to magazines, before and/or after publication as provided in specific contracts. They encourage book clubs to buy certain books. They promote books on the Internet. They may buy advertising, especially to small target groups where the advertising is more affordable. And they arrange author appearances at bookshops.

Inside the publishing industry, in ways that often aren't apparent to authors, publishers are busy encouraging bookshops to buy certain books. They give extra information to sales reps, publish articles and buy ads in trade magazines, and pay for special promotions.

Finally, publishers work out advertising arrangements with bookshops, especially the large national chains. For example, your publisher may help pay for a national magazine ad for a bookshop chain, with the understanding that several of their books will be featured in the ad. Or they may contribute money to a bookshop's ad campaign with the understanding that the bookshop will promote an author's appearance, or will place a particular book in a prominent position in the shop for a week or two. Books that are displayed on the tables in the front of the shop, or on the ends of aisles with their covers out, are often there as the result of a deal struck with the publisher.

For books they hope will be very big, a publisher might provide bookshops with a special display box for a book, one that sits on the floor or on the counter near the register, often called a 'dumpbin'.

In your promotion meeting, ask about all of these possibilities. See what your publisher has in mind or might be willing to consider.

ACCOMPLISH WHATEVER YOU CAN BEFORE YOUR PUBLICATION DATE

Now that you have a marketing plan and you know how your publisher plans to support you, proceed with your plan. Maybe you will be booking speaking engagements for yourself after the book comes out. Maybe you will be preparing a press pack to mail to radio and TV producers. Maybe you will be preparing a flier or postcard.

If your plan includes media, you may want to work with a media trainer for one or two sessions, or write up 'sound bites' and practice them. Maybe you will be locating mailing lists and preparing a mail-out for a direct mail campaign.

Whatever you have decided to do, the moment your book shows up in bookshops, *be ready* to launch it in the best possible way you can, given your resources. Get ready for that great Publication Day!

Celebrate Your Publication Date and Your Power As a Published Author

Time required: A day, an evening or a weekend to celebrate; the rest of your life to be a published writer.

CONSIDER A PUBLICATION EVENT

Events related to your book's publication occur over a period of several weeks. Probably the most exciting for you is the day you first receive a copy of your beloved book. Your editor will send you one as soon as it is off the presses. Shortly afterwards, you will receive a box of books, your 'author copies'. Pile them up and take pictures. Send a copy to your mum and your Aunt Tillie. Or just sit in a warm, cosy spot and read your masterpiece. Savour what a fine job you did!

While all this is going on in your living room, bookshops all over the country are receiving boxes of your books, letting them sit in the store room for a few days because the buyer has the flu or the bookshop is understaffed at the moment, and then unpacking them, inventorying them, and putting them out on their shelves – with the cover facing out, you hope.

The actual 'publication date' is a date when, if all goes according to plan, the books are on the shelves of bookshops all over the country, and your publicity for the book can begin. If a portion of your royalty advance is due upon publication, the publication date is the day your publisher will begin to think about generating your cheque. Expect it within a month or so.

Sometimes your publication date provides you with an opportunity to create a major publicity event. For a cookbook, for example, maybe they will throw a party in a famous restaurant. Usually, however, such a party is far more trouble and expense than it is worth. There are no guarantees that journalists and book reviewers who have been invited to your book launch party will show up; even if they do, they may not choose to write about your book afterwards.

Of course, you can plan your own celebration. Some publishers may be prepared to contribute towards the cost of a launch party, towards the cost of the refreshments, or the invitations, and will be happy to help you draw up a list of possible invitees. If you have personal connections in the media, or with anyone whose support might help you sell copies of your book, add their names to the list. Combine this 'official' launch party with a celebration to thank all the friends, relatives and colleagues who have supported you. Don't let the publication of your first book slip away unnoticed. If you can give your friends the opportunity to celebrate with you – and do some useful networking at the same time – then your launch party will be well worth the planning.

Whatever you decide to do to mark publication, congratulations! You are a published author! I'm excited with you and for you!

SUPPORT INDEPENDENT BOOKSELLERS

Huge bookshop chains like Waterstones and Dillons and (of course) the ubiquitous WH Smith are a fact of life in today's marketplace. Consumers like them because they are large, well-stocked and occupy easily accessible sites on virtually every High Street or shopping mall. And, because they have such a large share of the market, they are able to persuade publishers to offer them particularly advantageous terms, meaning that they can pass sizeable discounts on bestselling titles on to their customers. (Since the demise of the Net Book Agreement in 1995 – the agreement which meant booksellers had to sell books at the cover price set down by the publisher – discounting has been the order of the day.)

However, the growth of bookshop chains during the 1980s revolutionised the publishing industry in ways that were not necessarily advantageous to writers.

Their worse offence was to make bestsellers into a virtual cult and to minimise their marketing of the hundreds of books that are extremely high quality but don't happen to be blockbusters. Bookshop chains will devote far more space and energy to a book supported by a lavish marketing campaign – posters, dumpbins, authors tours – and, as you know, publishers are prepared to spend that sort of money on a book only if they are convinced that it is going to be a bestseller. Bookshop chains are all about profit. For them, books are products just like a tin of beans in a supermarket – and they need to sell large quantities of that product to be successful.

For the 99 per cent of us authors who write wonderful books that aren't necessarily bestsellers, these industry trends are bad news, and a far cry from the days when independent booksellers had far more influence in the industry.

However, the news is not all bad. Against the odds, some of the more enterprising and professional independent booksellers have continued to survive and even to thrive – and though they may not be able to sell books in such huge numbers as a branch of WH Smith, and cannot match the discounts on bestselling books that high-volume bookshop chains can give, they can offer authors mutual benefits and rewards.

Independent booksellers tend to be in the business because they love books. Otherwise, they would have chosen a business with a much higher profit margin on each item. They love building relation-ships with authors, supporting and encouraging them. They are generally happy to stock a wider range of books because they want to support a broad spectrum of writing. They relish the critical role they play in the industry, and they love supporting the best that publish-ers have to offer. They are likely to respond personally and with passion to customers' requests and take pleasure in recommending books to readers.

As writers we can do a great deal to support the independent bookshops that have fought off the onslaught of the big chains. Patronise them, and encourage your friends to do the same. Become friendly with the owners. Attend any special events they organise. They will do a great deal for you in return. You will find that local bookshops are particularly kindly disposed towards authors who live in their area and that they will be more than happy to support your book's publication with a window or in-store display, or a bookshop signing at the time of the launch. While you are better placed than your publisher to make the overtures to independent booksellers in these situations – after all, you are literally on their doorstep – your publisher will usually be delighted to help with anything you have set up, providing display showcards, extra copies of the book, etc. But do let your publicist at the publishing house know the details of exactly what you are planning so that she can discuss it with the bookseller. Don't make wild promises to the bookseller about what your publishers will be prepared to do for you and don't discuss payment terms; that must remain the responsibility of your publisher's sales department.

Amy Tan says: 'I owe my career to the independents. They hand-sold *The Joy-Luck Club* by saying to readers: "Here's a book you should read." The chains didn't buy it until six weeks after it had been on the bestseller list. The independents take a risk with a new author.'

This doesn't mean that you should ignore the bookshop chains! Do nurture relationships with the staff who work at these branches and encourage them to keep your book in stock. If you say that you have a strong local following and that there is likely to be a demand (and you can prove it), they will take notice. Book chains like Waterstones and Dillons are particularly good at organising literary events like readings and signings, often involving a group of authors rather than just one. If they know your name and know that you have a fan base in the neighbourhood who are likely to come along (and buy books), they may well include you in their plans.

BOOK FAIRS

Before I go any further, I should point out that book fairs exist primarily so that publishers can sell rights to other publishing companies. As a rule, most authors never get the chance to become officially involved in book fairs. Only the very biggest books of the year, written by those who are already celebrities and will therefore generate publicity on a global scale, tend to be promoted on this scale.

Book fairs are held annually. The two main book fairs for UK publishers are held in London in the spring and Frankfurt in the autumn – with a children's book fair in Bologna. Hundreds, perhaps thousands, of national and international publishers hire stands at the fairs to display their current and forthcoming lists – they are strictly forbidden actually to sell books. Then they hold back-to-back meetings with US and foreign rights representatives from other countries in the hope of negotiating rights deals on those books where they control rights. They do sometimes hold an author-led event at these book fairs with the aim of pushing their major title for the season. However, be warned that they will already have decided long before the fair is held which author they want to promote in this manner and will want to pour all their efforts into his or her particular book. They will probably discourage you from attending the fair unless they were planning to invite you in any case.

You won't gain a great deal from making your own arrangements to attend the Frankfurt Book Fair – apart from sore feet and a huge hole in your pocket. Frankfurt is prohibitively expensive and absolutely vast; if you spend a week there you will only have explored the tip of the iceberg. You will most likely come away feeling discouraged that there are so many books apart from yours in the world! However, it might just be worth your paying a visit to the London Book Fair, if only to see what sort of competition your book is likely to be up against when it is eventually published. London is smaller and friendlier than Frankfurt – and significantly cheaper – and it will certainly help you to get a handle on what sorts of books are doing well in the UK and how publishers are marketing them.

Publicise and Promote
Your Book

Time required: Ideal: Almost full time for three months;
part-time for one full year.
(Also effective: As much time as you have.)

Now you will begin to execute the promotion plan you have been putting in place for the last nine months. You may be conducting radio and TV interviews, making bookshop appearances, giving lectures or workshops, writing articles, beginning a direct mail campaign, placing advertisements, or dozens of other specialised activities you have cleverly devised.

Here are several suggestions that will increase your chances of success.

KEEP BOOKSELLERS POSTED

Part of the value of keeping yourself and your book in the public eye as much as you can is to convince booksellers to keep your book stocked. So you have to let them know everything you are doing.

How?

SALES REPS

The most obvious, direct route is your sales reps. These are the people stationed all over the country who are your publisher's direct liaisons with booksellers. Their job is to do whatever they can to persuade booksellers to keep your book stocked (along with the several hundred other books they represent). When you provide them with information about everything you are doing to promote your book, their job is easier.

The sales reps' 'boss' is the sales director. Your link with the sales director is your editor. So first, see whether you can establish a good relationship with your sales director. If possible, meet her. Then, as you conduct your promotion campaign, send your editor periodic memos, apprising her of all you have planned and are accomplishing, and any especially successful interviews or events. (Always send copies of the memos to your agent.) I suggest mail for these memos rather than fax or e-mail. Your editor and agent are faxed and e-mailed to distraction and become easily annoyed by too much of it from one person. Fax and e-mail demand their immediate attention and convey an urgency you don't intend.

If all goes according to plan, your editor will ensure the sales director receives all your memos. Then, the sales director will pass your information along to all the sales reps who will pass it along to booksellers, and booksellers will reorder your book.

Try to become acquainted with your publisher's sales rep in your own region. Your editor will tell you who it is. Call the person and see whether you can take him or her to lunch. Often, your rep will be too busy, but at least you can have a phone conversation. Then, especially when you are doing events in your local area, you can send special memos to your local rep, with copies to your sales director, editor and agent.

Definitely keep your editor supplied with information about all you are doing to promote your book, so he or she can inform sales reps, but don't rely exclusively on them. They are busy. They represent hundreds of books. The sales reps can't call every bookseller every time you make a radio appearance.

So next you need to think of ways to contact booksellers directly.

BOOKSHOP VISITS

For starters, visit as many booksellers as you possibly can. Set aside a few days to visit all the major bookshops in your local area, and visit as many as you can whenever you are on the road for any reason.

Whenever possible, phone the bookshops at least five days in advance to let them know you will be visiting. Ask to speak to the manager or buyer, and say something like, 'I just wanted to let you know I will be in the area and will be dropping by. I will be happy to sign any of my books you have available.' Often, the bookshop will be delighted you called and will specially order extra books so they have plenty for you to sign. This is one of the main results you hope for. But even if all that doesn't come together, it is still valuable to visit bookshops and introduce yourself to the buyer or manager and any staff who are there. If you leave a good impression, they will think of you the next time a customer asks for a book on your topic. When they are shelving books, they will put yours face out. Every little bit helps!

Consider bringing along a little gift for the staff, something related to your book. Harvey Mackay used to hand out little gold shark pins to advertise *Swim with the Sharks*. If your book is on romance, you might give the manager a little bag of chocolate hearts. Or leave a stack of bookmarks or fliers you have had made up about your book for customers to pick up off the counter.

You might want to carry around (removable) stickers that say 'Signed by the author' for the cover of the book, in case the bookseller doesn't have any. One author I know always had copies of his book with him, so if the bookshop was out of stock, he would sell or sometimes give the bookshop copies right there on the spot.

Don't take up a lot of the bookseller's time, but be enthusiastic about your book. Politely ask whether they would consider putting it in the window, especially if you are in town only for a day or two to do media appearances, and whether they would be willing to place the book on a display table or to display it with its cover facing out.

Concentrate on independent booksellers first, because chains do a lot of ordering nationally over which local branches have little control, but if you have time, visit the big chains too.

But unless you can take six months off, fill a van with your books, and head for the motorway, you won't be able to visit more than a handful of shops, relatively speaking. How else can you contact booksellers?

PHONE CALLS AND POSTCARDS

Once when I was scheduled to appear on a major regional TV programme, I photocopied the 'Bookshops' section of all the Yellow Pages in my region, rounded up ten friends, divided up the lists, and we telephoned every bookshop in five counties. First we asked to speak to the buyer or manager. Then we'd say, 'I wanted to let you know that Susan Page, author of *If I'm So Wonderful, Why Am I Still Single?*, is appearing on "People Are Talking" two weeks from today. We thought you might want to stock up on her book.' Most booksellers saw the phone call as a favour and appreciated it. After the show, I called the largest book wholesaler, and they reported a definite blip in orders from my area.

If you have lots of money, you can pay someone to telephone bookshops well ahead of your media appearances in a given town or city, to give them plenty of time to stock up on books.

Consider doing a mailing to bookshops, one city at a time, announcing your media appearances and the merits of your book.

OTHER IDEAS

If you, or a publicist you hire, books you for a major national TV or radio appearance, or a major newspaper or magazine article, and, if you know about it well in advance (often not the case, unfortunately), your publisher will probably be very good about getting the word out to bookshops. Check with your editor to see how they plan to do this.

Make booksellers your best friends. Whatever you can think of to support them, and to encourage and excite them about your book, do it. Independent booksellers especially are often asked for suggestions about books. Make your book the one that is in the front of their minds.

GUARD AGAINST THE FATAL GAP

The Fatal Gap is every author's worst nightmare: You get booked on *This Morning with Richard and Judy*. Or a publicist gets you a phenomenal ten media appearances in one city over two days. You arrive. Your show or all your media appearances are sensational. You are flushed with excitement. Then you learn from your publisher, or by going into bookshops yourself, that your books are nowhere to be found.

A media appearance does you very little good if your book is not in bookshops. While the public might be very keen to rush out and buy your book immediately after they hear you, two weeks later, when the books finally arrive, they will have forgotten all about you.

There are two times when the Fatal Gap is most likely to occur. One is at the very beginning of your media blitz when timing is tricky. You or a publicist must send out information before your books are actually distributed so that when copies do hit the stores, your media is already set up. The press release will say that this author is available after a certain date, but if a TV producer has a cancellation, and has your press pack in her hand, she may call you and say, 'If you are available the day after tomorrow, we'd love to talk to you about your book.' Do you tell the producer, 'Thanks, but we'd prefer to do it in three weeks?' You could try, but of course you risk losing the appearance altogether.

Go ahead and do the show. It won't do you any harm. You can add it to your résumé. But its effect on book sales will not be what it might have been if books were available at the time. Just one more piece of good news/bad news all wrapped up in one package.

The second time the Fatal Gap sometimes occurs is when booksellers sell the first books they ordered and then fail to order replacements. Especially if a book catches on swiftly because of one sensational media appearance or review, or because of an unanticipated demand, booksellers may be caught short. A worse variation on this theme occurs when your publisher sells out of its first printing quickly and lags behind with its second printing. Both of these are exasperating situations, and what I can suggest to prevent them is no guarantee of success.

With regard to the bookshops reordering, stay in touch with your booksellers as much as possible, as I have suggested above. If you have advance notice that you will be in a city doing publicity, telephone a representative sampling of bookshops to let them know you'll be there and to see whether the book is in stock. If you discover that most bookshops are out, alert your editor and agent. (Now you *do* have an urgent situation in which e-mail, fax or the good old phone is appropriate.) If you are assured that your editor is going to leap into action, ask her if there is anything you can do to support her. If you feel she is preoccupied with other things and doesn't view this situation as a crisis, another step you might take is to call the wholesalers – you should have taken care to find out from your publisher's sales department who they do business with. Ask to speak to the buyer who deals with your publishing house. Tell that individual about the crisis to be sure that he has plenty of books on hand when the booksellers start calling, asking for your book in a panic.

The best way to manage the awful circumstance of your publisher running out of its first print run is to try to prevent it to begin with. Stay on top of sales figures as I suggest below. Keep your editor apprised of everything you are doing to market your book. If your promotion is going extremely well – interviewers seem to want you, you are getting good reviews – start asking early about the second print run. Be sure your agent is fully involved. Let her begin to agitate for a large and early second printing.

Print-run sizes are a Catch-22. Early on, your publisher decides where on their 'list' your book will be. If it is one of their top books for the season, they will print a lot of books, the reps will push it as a top book to get it well distributed, and the publisher will give it a big promotion budget. *Of course* that book will do better than a 'mid-list' book for which they do a smaller print run and less promotion. There is a lot of self-fulfilling prophecy that goes on in this business. The Fatal Gap will occur if your own promotion campaign is way above average, and the book sells better than the publisher predicted it would and positioned it to.

Of course with most books, publishers' predictions come true, the number of books they print is sufficient, steady sales do prompt booksellers to reorder, and publishers have a ready supply of books. The Fatal Gap never occurs.

I wish I could provide a better solution to the problem when it does occur. I fear the best I can do is to alert you to it. The reality is, if you plan an extraordinary marketing and promotion effort, you must also convince your publisher and booksellers to support you by keeping books in the marketplace. A good strong agent will be a big help here. Good luck!

MONITOR YOUR SALES FIGURES

Everyone in your life who has been following the adventure of your book will be asking you, 'How is your book doing?' No one wants to know the answer more than you. But another strange quirk of the publishing industry is that they behave as though this is vague, elusive, unknowable information and that, in any case, it is not important for you to know.

If you have to wait for your first royalty statement to learn what your sales are, you may be waiting a long time. Royalty statements are only issued twice annually, at set times (typically, October and April).

Sales figures are available. Sales reps have to know what has been ordered and sold in order to know what to encourage booksellers to buy. Publishers' computer systems are improving. In many houses now, sales information can be accessed easily by every editor.

So don't sit around and wait for someone to call you and tell you how many of your books are selling. Ask. First ask your editor. She will be able to tell you how many of your books were ordered by bookshops before it was published. Then, as you are proceeding with your promotion plan, she should be able to tell you how many books have been reordered.

Wait for eight weeks after your publication date. If you have heard nothing about sales, ask your editor. If she acts as though this is classified information, or that it is only a vague concept and nobody really has any idea, ask your agent to intervene for you. If you have a relationship with the sales rep in your area, see if you can get an answer from that person. Or see if the sales director will speak with you.

Or, again, call a book wholesaler. See if you can connect with a friendly person there who will give you sales information every six weeks or so. Begin by asking for the person who buys books from your publisher, but, especially with smaller wholesalers, any friendly person might be willing to help you.

UNDERSTAND THAT THE EFFECT OF PUBLICITY IS CUMULATIVE

It is easy to fall into the belief that, after it's all said and done, publicity and promotion don't really accomplish all that much. You spend five minutes doing a radio interview. You hang up, and, even if you are very pleased with what you said in five minutes, you think, 'Out of the one hundred people who heard this, thirty of them are going to drop everything and rush out and buy my book. Not likely. Why am I bothering with all this?' It's easy to become discouraged, because you will rarely experience immediate results from any one piece of promotion you do.

This attitude is understandable, but it is completely misguided. Publicity works. Otherwise, publishers wouldn't continue to spend millions of pounds doing it.

First of all, it sometimes is true that a person will hear one interview or read one article and then rush out and buy your book. That's why book sales can soar the week after an author appears on TV, or is mentioned in the press. Such sales surges don't *automatically* happen anymore: sometimes, but not always.

But more often, publicity works because its effect is cumulative. One radio spot by itself wouldn't sell your book. But if a listener hears your five minutes on the radio, then three weeks later sees a good review of your book, then notices an advertisement for one of your workshops, then a week later overhears someone talking about your book, and a week after that sees it in a bookshop, by then, that person may be ready to buy. Bear in mind that John Gray's very successful *Men Are from Mars, Women Are from Venus* didn't appear on the best-seller list until nine months after it was published.

My main point here is that your attitude will make an enormous difference in how successful your publicity is. If you *believe* you are making a difference with every effort you make, no matter how small, you will make all those efforts with the kind of determination that succeeds. But if you believe that all you are doing is an exercise in futility, it may end up being just that.

I have heard authors complain bitterly about how exhausting an author tour is, the kind where the publisher sends you to a new town every day for a week and plans radio, TV and press interviews for you all day long. What an opportunity such a tour is! But you have to attack it with zeal, or the opportunity will be lost.

Not all books succeed the way their authors hope they will – and believe they should. Sometimes a book's moderate (instead of sensational) success is unexplainable. Nevertheless, I believe it is safe to say that commitment, enthusiasm and a strong belief in both your book and in the potential of your promotion plan are fundamental requirements for success.

PREPARE FOR YOUR MEDIA INTERVIEWS

Of all the advice I have received and lessons I've learned the hard way about how to give excellent radio and TV interviews, I consider the following suggestions to be the most useful:

1. FOCUS ON THREE POINTS

Whether your interview is three minutes or a full hour, you cannot distil the contents of your entire book for your listeners. Let go of that most natural desire. Give it up.

Instead, carefully select three points. Each one should be innovative and different from what we've all heard before, genuinely useful, informative, or entertaining for your listeners, and easy to introduce in a 'sound bite' (the one or two sentences you will be able to spew out before the interviewer asks you another question or cuts you off for a commercial). Your aim is to intrigue your listeners and to leave them hungry for more.

For each of your three points, write out and memorise three to five sentences that make the point clearly. That's the sound bite. In addition, have in mind one or two short, memorable, wisdom-filled anecdotes or examples that illustrate each of your three points. Practice delivering your anecdotes succinctly.

Finally, give each point one key word, and put those three words in the front of your brain, saying them over and over to yourself, just before your interview begins.

Now, no matter what question comes at you, you will have something completely ready to say without having to sift mentally through your whole book. You will be able to deliver each point briefly and to stop talking when you have made it. Silence makes you appear confident, authoritative and professional, whereas endless chatter can muddy your message and annoy your interviewer. An additional advantage of the three-point system is that, whether you were able to convey one, two or even three of your beloved points, you can feel confident that the interview was a success – even though you didn't get to talk about your whole book.

Of course, you do not have to limit yourself to your three points. You will be asked many questions for which you have ready answers because you know your material so well. But with your three points, whenever you have an opportunity to take initiative, you'll be ready. And you will be able to leap in quickly with an answer to a general question, of which interviewers are very fond, especially at the beginning of the interview when you want to make your best impression.

When my first book, *If I'm So Wonderful, Why Am I Still Single?*, was first published, as it turned out, my very first media interview ever of any kind was . . . *Oprah*! Even my publisher must have been a little nervous, because they sent me to a media trainer. I will be forever grateful that I learned the 'three key words' technique from her.

Twenty-four hours later, I was seated on Oprah's stage, along with three other guests. Oprah made a few opening comments about the plight of singles today, and then, without notice, whirled around and said, 'Well, let me ask our guests. What do you think is the biggest problem singles face today?'

If I hadn't been prepared with only three words in the front of my brain, I would have had to sift through dozens of possibilities: They have to deal with terrible statistics? The rules of dating are all changing? There is no good way to meet people? Men and women want different things? – All subjects I deal with in the book. All interesting topics.

But I didn't even have to think. Without a moment's hesitation, I leaped into the void with one of my three points:

'Singles are ambivalent about what they really want, because singlehood has a lot of appeal, but so does marriage, so singles are always sabotaging themselves. If you don't know where you are going, every road seems like the wrong one.'

It's the one point that I believe sets my work apart from others. It intrigued Oprah, so she asked more about it. It made me seem authoritative and knowledgeable. And I got to speak first!

Don't leave home without your three key words!

2. BE LIKEABLE

Your book is so rich and fascinating that you will be frustrated because you can touch upon such a tiny fraction of it. Relax. As it turns out, just as important as the information you convey is the general impression you create. Rather than looking frustrated when the interviewer cuts you off in the middle of a brilliant point, laugh it off. Smile a lot. Be warm, animated and full of energy. Warm up to the interviewer, even if you don't especially like him or her. If the audience feels that you are gracious, mature, confident and wise, they will *remember* you and want to become better acquainted with you by buying your book.

To be sure, the information you are able to give should be very interesting. But your listeners are likely to forget what you say. They are more likely to remember the general impression you give. Relax and be yourself (unless you are a dry, boring or irritable person). Have a good time. Be assured that whatever you are able to say about your book is enough.

3. USE ANECDOTES

Points are easily forgotten. Wonderful stories stay in people's brains for a long time. Prepare several short but wonderful stories that illustrate your main points or introduce a character, and try to use at least one of them in each interview. Sometimes, you won't be able to squeeze it in, or it won't be appropriate. But whenever you can make a point with a story, your audience is more likely to remember you, and to like you.

4. LEARN TO BRIDGE

Especially on radio phone-in shows, you may be asked questions that have nothing to do with what you want to talk about. Sometimes, even interviewers lead you far from the points you want to make.

Remember that coming across as a friendly, approachable person is as important as any one point you want to make, so take your caller seriously. At least briefly, answer the question directly. But then, with your three points smack in the front of your mind, glide over to a point that *you* want to make and that you think will be of greater interest to most of your listeners. Media coaches call this 'bridging', gracefully moving from one subject to another without being too obvious about it.

Here's an example. Suppose you are being interviewed about direct mail marketing and one of your three points is that you have to follow up immediately with customers who respond to your mailing. The interviewer asks, 'What percentage of unsolicited direct mail gets thrown away unopened?' Of course, you have no interest in dwelling on this negative aspect of your business. In fact, the question could even be viewed as a bit hostile. You might be tempted to respond like this:

> 'Well, you know, it doesn't matter what percentage gets thrown away. We focus only on the percentage that does get opened. Depending on the subject matter and how well the audience was targeted, anywhere from 2 to 15 per cent may open the mailing. If the mailing is extremely targeted, as many as 50 per cent may open it.'

But then the interviewer is likely to ask you another question about unopened mail, and you are off in a difficult direction. Worse, the precious moments you have to make the points *you* want to make are ebbing away.

Here is an example of a response that is polite but that bridges to one of your three main points:

> 'It's surprising to a lot of people who have never used direct mail that only 2 to 15 per cent of the mail gets opened,

depending on how targeted the mailing is. But look at it this way: If you use the most important strategy, which is to follow up immediately on each response you do receive, you can easily *double* the number of new customers you would normally get in a month – just by doing a small mailing! You'd be surprised at how many of the people who respond to a mailing will end up becoming your customers, *if* they receive the information they have requested in a timely manner. Waiting too long to respond is the biggest mistake novice direct mail marketers make.'

You will become better at bridging as you are able to practice. Bridging allows you to have more control over your interview and puts you less at the mercy of irrelevant questions.

Here are several other phrases, useful for bridging:

'I'm not sure I can answer that, but I can tell you . . .'

'If you're asking whether (insert a question you prefer to discuss) . . .'

'People ask me that a lot, and they also ask about . . .'

5. DO NOT RELY ON NOTES

Trust me, you won't have time to refer to notes during an interview. If you will feel more confident with a few key words on an index card, there's no harm in having one card. You may be able to set it on a coffee table during a TV interview, and of course there's no problem taking notes into a radio studio. But keeping three points and stories in your head, and knowing you have a broad general knowledge of your subject you can draw on, will serve you much better than pages of notes on various topics. They will be useless.

6. DON'T BE OPENLY PROMOTIONAL, BUT BE SURE YOUR TITLE IS MENTIONED OFTEN

Don't rave about your book yourself. Don't refer readers to your book for the answer to a question, as in, 'I cover that in detail in Chapter Seven.' You can sometimes sneak in a line like, 'Of the three suggestions I offer in the book, let me discuss just one now.' But presenters and audiences alike will become annoyed with you if they detect that you are pushing your book.

Of course everyone knows that's why you are there. But the above-board reason you are there is to entertain and educate listeners. Give them all you possibly can in the time you have.

Most presenters are excellent about mentioning the title of your book numerous times throughout the interview, but if you notice this isn't happening, try to sneak it in unobtrusively yourself.

7. SPEAK IN THE FIRST OR SECOND PERSON; AVOID THIRD PERSON

Suppose your book is about learning to play the piano as an adult. Listen to a comment in the third person:

'When an adult first starts to play the piano, they usually feel overwhelmed until they realise they can take only one step at a time.'

Uses sloppy grammar, and sounds theoretical. Let's try using correct grammar:

'When an adult first starts to play the piano, he or she usually feels overwhelmed until he or she realises that he or she can only take one step at a time.'

You'll realise you are into a nightmare when you get halfway into the sentence, and you'll probably end up bumbling around. Besides, 'an adult' is a remote, mythical figure, not very personal or close to home.

Now listen to the second-person version:

'When you first start to play the piano as an adult, you usually feel a little overwhelmed, until you realise you can take only one step at a time.'

Personal, direct and fluent.
Or, it is usually appropriate to talk about yourself.

'When I first started to play the piano as an adult, I felt a little overwhelmed, until I realised I could take only one step at a time.'

First- and second-person speaking is more direct, more personal, more friendly, and far easier to negotiate. Whenever possible, tell a personal story or use the generic 'you'.

8. BRING EVERYTHING YOU WILL NEED

Always have these items with you:

A. Several Copies of Your Book.   This is especially important for TV for the rare occasions when they don't have a copy. Usually, you or the publicist who booked the interview will have sent the producer a copy. But mishaps happen. Be prepared.

B. A Page of Questions for the Interviewer.   Again, this will have been sent out with your promotion materials, and unfortunately, interviewers, in my experience, usually ignore your prepared questions anyway. But you never know when the interviewer will have become ill and a last-minute substitute who has never heard of you or your book has been supplied. I've even had interviewers who knew I was coming ask me for a list of questions.

I usually carry two pages. On one, I print just five or six questions in large type. These are questions for which I have prepared exquisite answers, and I list them in the order I want them to be asked. If the interviewer sticks to these questions in this order, it will be an ideal interview from my point of view. On the second page, I begin with those five or six but add another six or seven for a total of ten to fourteen questions.

C. A Page of Your Promotional Information for the Host.   Would you like the presenter to mention a Freephone number where viewers can order your book? Will you be offering a workshop tomorrow evening or giving a public lecture, and you want viewers to know the time and place? Will you be appearing at a local bookshop?

Print this information clearly, and hand it to the producer or presenter with a request that the information be mentioned on the air.

D. Aston Information.   As you are speaking on TV, often the station will identify you by displaying words at the bottom of the screen, called the aston. What would you like them to say after your name? It could be 'Childcare Expert', 'Small Business Owner', or, usually best if you are promoting a book, 'Author of *The Sex Life of Dinosaurs*'. Hand the producer a page with your name spelled correctly and the way you would like to be identified on the aston, should they be planning to use one.

E. Blank Audio and Video Cassette Tapes.   As soon as possible when you arrive at the station, ask your producer whether you will be able to obtain a copy of your segment of the programme. You are much more likely to get results if you supply a blank tape on the spot. Of the fifty or so producers who have told me, 'We'll mail you a dub later,' I have received maybe five. But I'm usually successful when I hand the producer a blank tape. For short segments, you can put several on the same tape. Just ask the producer not to rewind, and start your new segment where the last one left off.

Tapes of your media appearances are valuable for two reasons. First, you will improve your interviews by watching or listening to yourself. You are your own best critic. If you are working with a media trainer, or you decide to do so later on, the two of you can work with your tapes.

Second, use the best of your interviews to make up a demo tape to sell yourself to conference organisers who might be considering inviting you to speak; to other radio and TV producers; and to publishers of future books who want to know how you come across on radio and TV.

Especially if you plan to use your taped segments for a demo video, obtain Betacam SP blank tapes from a professional video supply house and carry them with you. Betacam tapes provide a higher quality reproduction than VHS tapes. And more important, they make it easier for a producer to accommodate your request for a copy of your segment. Betacam SP can easily be converted to VHS for home viewing.

9. BE PREPARED FOR A VARIETY OF INTERVIEW STYLES

The interviewers out there in TV and radio land vary greatly. As you'll find, a great deal of the success of an interview depends upon the skill and style of the interviewer. The best interviewers will have read your book, or a substantial portion of it. Their questions arise out of genuine interest in your subject. They make you feel as though you are in a conversation with a friend or client who truly cares about what you are saying and wants to know more.

Many interviewers will not have read your book, but they will have looked over your press materials and familiarised themselves with the general subject. If you are unlucky, they will have an axe to grind, and will want to dwell on one part of your topic that doesn't interest you. Sometimes, they will use the questions you have submitted to them in the press pack, but often with their own slant.

Occasionally an interviewer will be completely unprepared. If the person lets you take off on your own and control where you want to go, this can be okay. But sometimes their questions display their ignorance and are useless or even embarrassing.

Worst, of course, but very uncommon, is a hostile interviewer. If someone is antagonising you or disagrees with you, unless your topic is a political or social issue on which the audience will also be divided and everyone expects tempers to flare, remember: It is more important for you to make a good impression on your listeners than to win any points or get revenge on someone who is obviously being rude. Try to be the 'big' person in the situation. Don't become defensive. Acknowledge the interviewer's point of view, and gently repeat your own when you get a chance. It is okay to say things like, 'I can see you have some serious feelings on this topic,' or 'I can see you don't agree with me at all on this.' Diffuse the hostility, if possible, and don't play the game. You be the nice guy. Your audiences will appreciate your graciousness – and they'll remember you.

10. CONSIDER WORKING WITH A STYLE CONSULTANT AND A MEDIA TRAINER

I highly recommend at least one session with a style consultant before you appear on TV. Your appearance says a great deal about you before you even open your mouth, and TV cameras can be cruel. Television stations often provide their own make-up artists, but in case yours doesn't, a style consultant can tell you how to vary your usual make-up for the TV cameras. And coming up with an outfit that does everything you want it to can be a challenge. Do you want to appear warm, successful, professional or creative? These are all different looks. What colours bring out the best in you? Are you better in prints or solids? The old 'rules' about what to wear on TV are no longer as critical as decisions about what you want to say with your appearance. Even if you give your apparel no attention at all, and just throw on something from your wardrobe, you will be making a statement to your viewers. To maximise this opportunity, for which you have laboured so hard, ask a professional for some help. You may be amazed at the difference a style consultant can make. Don't let anything diminish your confidence or your impact.

A media trainer is less critical, especially now that I have filled you in on the basics. But don't hesitate to consult one if you are nervous about your upcoming interviews. Media consultants, most of whom are ex-journalists or presenters themselves, give you helpful suggestions about what to say and how to say it, how well you are conveying your core message, how you come across on camera, and how to appear more animated. They will alert you to any distracting gestures, phrases or habits you may be unaware of. Perhaps most helpful, they give you the opportunity to practice and to see yourself on tape so that you can make adjustments if you choose.

A media trainer may be most helpful to you after you have completed a round of interviews when you have specific questions and a clearer idea of exactly what you would like help with.

PERSEVERE

Among authors, there are those who love to write and tolerate the necessary promotion, and there are those who suffer through the writing so they can have the fun of promoting. And then there are those who enjoy both.

It doesn't matter which type you are; in order to keep writing, you have to promote your work. So, even if you don't love promoting, make the best of it. Find ways to promote your book that are suited to your personality and lifestyle, and make up your mind you are going to enjoy it. What works for me is to separate the two tasks as much as possible. When I'm promoting, I don't expect myself to write. And when I'm writing, I quieten down my promoting as much as possible.

The secret to success in promotion is commitment. Through all the hassles and the parts of it that you don't like, keep your eye on the goal: book sales! The more you believe in the potential of your book to help or move or entertain or educate people, the more zeal you will be able to conjure up to keep the promotion in motion. Your book and your life as a writer are worth it.

Royalty Cheques and Remainders

Time required: One to four hours.

ROYALTY STATEMENTS AND ROYALTY CHEQUES

Most book contracts state that you will receive a royalty statement and, if any money is due to you, a royalty cheque every six months. As we've said, you don't have to wait for the statement to find out how well your book is selling; your editor should be keeping you posted about that all along.

In the age of computers, it would seem that publishers should be able to generate royalty statements fairly quickly, but the industry standard is three months. So for the six-month period January to June, you will receive your royalty statement and cheque in early October, and so on.

Royalty statements are usually complicated and difficult for a lay person to understand. They take into account not just sales to book-shops, but sales to wholesalers, catalogues, book clubs, discount retailers and subsidiary rights sales, and other kinds of special sales, often at different prices. Then there is this annoying little feature called 'reserve against returns'.

The publishing industry is the only retail business in the world that allows retailers to purchase merchandise and then return what they don't sell. It works in publishing because otherwise, booksellers would have to be extremely conservative about what they buy, and they would have to wait ages before having enough room on their shelves for new books. What this practice means to you is that when the publisher has sold 5,000 of your books to bookshops, you can't be sure they are really sold, because three months or a year later, the bookshop might return them and ask for a refund. So even though your royalty statement might say that you have sold 5,000 books, the publisher doesn't want to pay you for that many until they are certain some of them won't be returned. So they figure out what they owe you according to all those complicated percentages you signed months ago in your contract, and then they deduct a certain percentage as a 'reserve against returns'. This should be no more than 15 per cent of the royalties on the hardcover edition, or 25 per cent on a paperback. They should only be entitled to withhold this reserve at the first accounting date following publication and must undertake to pay you the balance owing if returns are not made.

If you don't understand your royalty statement, ask your agent to talk you through it until you do. Take notes so that you won't have to have this same conversation again in six months. After two or three royalty statements, you'll start to get the hang of it.

REMAINDERS

Some time after the publication of your book in hardcover or paperback, sales will have slowed or ceased altogether. At this point the publisher has to decide whether it is worth keeping quantities of unsold books in its warehouse or whether to sell them off to a discount book dealer at a very low price. You should insist that this does not happen until your book has been in the marketplace for at least a year, as it may well be that the publicity you are continuing to generate will allow book sales suddenly to take off.

If you are informed that the time has come for your book to be remaindered, you should be given first refusal on the remaining stock. If you sell books at workshops, conferences and similar events, you may welcome the chance to buy a large quantity of your books at a dramatically discounted price since you will be able to sell them at the cover price and thus make a good profit on each book.

You should also give your written consent for remaindering to take place and you should receive 10 per cent of the net receipts of any discounted sales made by the publishers of remaindered stock.

Participate in Your Paperback Publication and Start Planning Your Next Book

Time required: Three to ten hours of letters and phone calls.

THE PAPERBACK REPRINT OF YOUR HARDCOVER

If your book was published in hardcover, usually about one year after its initial publication date, your publisher will want to reprint it as a paperback. As we discussed before, the shelf life of the average hardcover book is about three months. After that, booksellers are looking to clear shelf space for a new batch of hardcovers. That's why the first three months of your book's life are the most critical time for heavy promotion.

If your book is selling at all well, bookshops may keep it in stock for a full year. But then, they and thousands of readers who decided not to buy it until it comes out in paperback will be eager to say bye-bye to your precious hardcover. In fact, you may welcome this change too. It will make your book available to far more people. And because the new format makes it 'news' again, it will give you a whole new opportunity to approach the media for interviews.

THE SALE

Virtually always, the hardcover publisher retains the right to decide when and how to publish the paperback. If the original deal you struck with them was a 'hard-soft' deal, it means they have already paid you for the right to reprint the book in paperback. If your original deal was hardcover only, they may elect to publish the paperback themselves, in which case they will need to pay you a new royalty advance, which your agent will negotiate for you, or they may elect to sell the paperback rights to another publisher (less likely nowadays).

Your agent will keep you informed about the paperback plans. But there is little you can do to influence them. Usually, between your agent and your hardcover editor, they will make a very good decision on your behalf. They will decide whether to publish a 'trade' (quality) paperback or a mass market paperback.

THE COVER

Once the format is decided, I suggest you leap into action.

The usual procedure is that the author is left completely out of everything having to do with the publication of the paperback. One day, you will collect the post and find a copy of your new paperback with a little note saying 'Congratulations!' If you are lucky, you will like the cover. If you aren't, you may be lukewarm about their design or extremely unhappy with it. All you can do is sob for two days, rail at the stupidity and injustice of their not consulting you, dry your tears and resolve to make the best of it.

Do your very best to avert this scenario. Here are my suggestions:

1. Find out who your new paperback editor is – this may be the same person who handled the hardcover edition of your book – and call him up. Introduce yourself, say how pleased you are, and ever so sweetly say that you would appreciate being kept in the loop as cover design and copy decisions get made. Realise that they will see this as an unusual idea and may not be prepared to agree to it right away. No matter what happens, be understanding and friendly.

2. Immediately, write up the promotional copy you would like to see on the back cover of the book. Include your most powerful endorsements. Include a fabulous strap headline – what is known as a 'shoutline'. Definitely include five to eight bullet points summarising the most distinctive, most important content of the book. What do you want the cover to say about you, the author? Keep that part brief, just two or three sentences. Look at the paperback version of the books that are your closest competitors in the marketplace. Be sure your copy sounds more exciting and enticing than theirs. If at all possible, work with a professional advertising or promotional copywriter.

Second, review what I said in Step 14 about the cover design memo, and write one of those. What do you like or not like about the hardcover design? What do you think the design of the paperback needs to accomplish? In what specific ways must your design distinguish your book from your close competitors'? If you think it is important or useful, enclose the covers of books you are competing with. Do you want to suggest specific colours or design ideas? Would you like the book to co-ordinate with other paperbacks you have out? Would you like it to have the same look as the hardcover? Or is this a chance to start again?

Third, make a complete list of all the endorsements and reviews you have received for the book, including any you have received since the hardcover was published and any your hardcover publisher elected not to use. Suggest that they might consider printing all the endorsements and an excerpt from each review on the front few pages of the book.

Now send your paperback editor a letter saying that you are enclosing your suggestions for the cover design and copy and that you hope they will be helpful. Again, ask him whether he would be willing to send you their design in time for you to make suggestions about it.

Of course, send a copy of everything to your agent.

Ten days after you send the letter, if you have heard nothing, phone the editor. First talk with the editor's assistant. Make friends with that person if you haven't already. Ask what she knows about the status of your letter. If she reassures you that the editor has seen it and possibly even commented favourably about it, that's enough. If the assistant waffles, ask to speak with the editor. Be very respectful of his time. Just check to see whether he received your letter and whether he seemed favourably disposed toward it. Gently mention again that you look forward to reviewing the cover before it is final. Since this is not their customary procedure, you need to be persistent, but work very hard above all to be polite and nice, and not to even suggest that you might become demanding or turn yourself into a nuisance. When you cross that line, your publishers will stop caring what you think. They have worked with too many thoughtless, pushy authors. Professional, mutually respectful participation is what you seek.

In the end, they may or may not use your suggestions. Especially if you did not work with a professional advertising or promotional copywriter, their marketing staff may be able to improve greatly on what you submitted, and as soon as you see it, you will agree. Maybe you will love the design they submit. Maybe you will like it but have a suggestion or two.

Whatever happens, if you have at the very least been able to persuade your editor to let you see the cover before it is final, you will be able to remove anything you view as a disaster or ask them to add some critical element they have left off. Seeing the finished product when you are helpless to make any changes can be infuriating. Why publishers do it this way, I don't understand. Maybe you and I working together can gradually effect a change.

START PLANNING YOUR NEXT BOOK

Congratulations! Now you can collect £200, return to GO, and start the whole journey all over again. If you have had a satisfying and successful enough experience writing your first book, chances are you will be eager to do another one.

Second books sometimes present a new set of questions. Let me answer two of the most common:

Q: I'm unhappy with my agent. Can I find a new one for my second book?
A: Yes. Your contract with your agent will probably contain a clause saying that either of you can end your working arrangement by giving thirty to ninety days' written notice. Of course, your first agent will still receive her percentage in perpetuity on everything she has accomplished so far with your first book. But if she has not yet sold foreign rights, for example, she may be willing to release that task and the remuneration that goes with it to your new agent.

It is probably wise not to terminate your association with your first agent until a new agent has agreed to work with you. You will need to search for the new agent using exactly the same method I have suggested in Step 9, using your new proposal for your second book. Be open with any new agent regarding your relationship with agent 1. Chances are, the new agent will be content with an explanation like, 'The relationship wasn't working out.' Or you may want to be more specific. For example, 'I felt she wasn't aggressive enough.' Be careful not to make it sound like you are a difficult author to work with.

The whole publishing industry, including most agents, operate on the principle 'if it works, keep doing it'. It's an understandable policy, but one that discourages change and may not match your needs. If you have just published a successful business book and now you want to write a book about horses, or you want to switch genres or change from non-fiction to fiction or vice-versa, your agent may give you a hard time because she knows she will have a tough time with editors. They will want you to continue along the lines you've begun and just won't be able to make the switch to a whole new arena. Bear in mind, your agent may be 100 per cent right in her recommendation. I might never have written my third relationship book without just that sort of encouragement. But if you are absolutely certain you are ready to make a change and your agent is not with you, consider finding a new agent.

Similarly, if your first book was published as a paperback original and you would like your second book to be published as a hardcover, this may be a hard switch for an agent to make.

If your agent has put you into a niche that you don't fit in anymore and you are unable to convince him or her that you are ready to move forward in a new way, you may be forced to change agents. One prolific writer told me she had to change agents several times for this reason. 'Every time I wanted to move up, I had to find a new agent,' she said.

Q: If my first book didn't do too well, will that affect the sale of my second book?

A: Possibly.

Of course, the reverse is certainly true: If your first book did extremely well, your second book sale is more likely to be easy and to earn you a substantial advance – if it is itself an excellent proposal. Notice I said, 'more likely'. Even if you are quite successful with your first book, your second sale might still be a challenge. Build on your success, but don't take anything for granted. You still have to do a superb job on your second proposal.

But if sales on your first book were average or below average, you will run smack into the latest industry pitfall, the one that has come to be known as 'the track', short for the track record you have established as an author. In recent years, computer advances have made sales records widely available, so it is harder than it once was for you and your agent to minimise your previous sales statistics.

A poor track record can be a serious handicap for a second sale. In fact, an *unknown* author may have a better chance at a good sale than an author whose first book sold poorly. I know of an author who received £50,000 for her first book and could get only £10,000 for her second because sales of the first book were disappointing. I recently heard an agent advise her client, only partly tongue-in-cheek, that he should consider writing his second book under a pseudonym, so that he wouldn't have a problem with his poor 'track'.

But there are signs that the industry is beginning to loosen up. Judging a potential book project by this single criterion is myopic and could be a big mistake. Editors are beginning to see this. An author with a poor first showing is likely to be both wiser and more highly motivated than a first-time author. Book promotion definitely has a learning curve. And all that aside, the second book may be a huge improvement over the first. It is an entirely different book that should be judged on its own merits!

If you are an author with a poor track record, your first job is to convince your agent to fight for you. If she is giving you the old story about 'the track', write her a letter. Use the arguments in the above paragraph. Being careful to avoid telling her how to do her job, provide her with ammunition. Remind her that the track should be only a minor consideration; this is an entirely new book, you now know a great deal more about how to promote and are more committed to it. Demonstrate your enthusiasm about and belief in your new project.

If you can persuade your agent to move beyond the 'track mentality', you have a good chance of knocking yourself out of this bunker and back onto the green. Be determined that it won't defeat you. Many of the world's most successful books were second or third books, including *Men Are from Mars, Women Are from Venus* by John Gray.

* * *

There you have the 20 Steps, from the first moment you had the idea to write a book to your paperback and on to future books. Here's hoping the whole process has been enjoyable and successful for you. I'd love to know how you feel about it all and what you have to add to what we've said. Be sure to see my note at the end of Part II about staying in touch with other writers and continuing this publishing dialogue.

Taming the Monsters and Reaping the Joy

Self-Doubt

Visualise your ideal life as a writer.

First there are the outer trappings: a cosy, private writing studio tucked among the trees. Five uninterrupted hours every day to write. A book contract that supports you for the next year. Publishers begging for your next book. A regular magazine column.

And then there is your ideal *inner* life as a writer: Every day, you have a clear idea of exactly what you are going to write. You sit down and the words flow effortlessly. Then you read what you've written and feel so much pleasure inside that you can barely contain your excitement. You absolutely know with deep certainty that this is outstanding work and have no doubt that an agent, editor and the public are going to be salivating for more of your genius. You love to write so much that you will happily make any sacrifices necessary to be able to continue your work.

I'm just guessing at your ideal writing life, of course. But it probably includes time and a place to write, passion about the process of writing, and unmitigated certainty about the high quality of the finished product.

Most of us aren't there yet. Instead, we are writing on the kitchen table or in an office designed primarily for something else. We write in hours stolen after everything else is completed. The writing itself is a struggle, and the finished product could be genius or sheer disaster; we are never quite sure. And we are terrified to show it to anyone to find out which.

Between the idea for a written piece and the completed, published piece lies a huge minefield of fears, unforeseen obstacles, setbacks, rejections and genuine doubt about your ability to write that I am grouping loosely under the term self-doubts. I've had the opportunity to explore this minefield for many years now and have learned something about the nature of these mines. I hope some of it will be useful to you.

GETTING TO COMMITMENT

In order to undertake any project as enormous as writing a book, you need commitment. In the well-worn quotation, often misattributed to Goethe but actually from *The Scottish Himalayan Expedition* by W. H. Murray, we hear great wisdom:

> Until one is committed, there is hesitancy, the chance to draw back, always ineffectiveness. Concerning all acts of initiative, there is one elementary truth, the ignorance of which kills countless ideas and endless plans:
>
> The moment [you] definitely commit [yourself], then Providence moves too. All sorts of things occur to help [you] that would never otherwise have occurred. A whole stream of events issues from the decision, raising in [your] favour all manner of unseen incidents and meetings and material assistance, which [you] could never have dreamed would come [your] way.
>
> > Whatever you can do or dream you can, begin it.
> > Boldness has genius, power, and magic to it.
> > > Goethe

(Goethe actually did write the last couplet.)

Inspiring! The problem is, how do you get to the point of being able to commit like that with your total soul if you just aren't there yet? It's a paradox: The universe doesn't start to move with you until you commit fully, but it is hard to commit fully until the universe gives you some sign that you are on the right track. In short, how do you become committed if you are filled with self-doubt?

First of all, I believe there are two types of commitment: intention-style commitment and burning commitment.

Intention-style commitment is something you manufacture in your head. You promise yourself or someone else that you will do a certain thing, let's say, write a book. You want to do it, and you make plans to do it. You might still be plagued with self-doubts, but you decide to go for it anyway.

Intention-style commitment doesn't bring all the forces of the universe with it. But it is a wonderful place to start.

Then you begin to work on your project. One of two things will happen: You will find that the project is hard work; it is not as easy or fun as you thought; and your interest will begin to flag. Or the more you get into the project, the more your excitement will build. If this happens, at some point, you will experience a dramatic inner shift, and your intention-style commitment will transform into burning commitment.

Burning commitment is the kind Murray was talking about, and the kind Napoleon Hill describes in his classic book *Think and Grow Rich*. It is a deep inner passion, a feeling of absolute certainty that nothing can stop you from achieving your goal. Burning commitment is not something you *decide* to have, it is something you *discover* is there. And it is truly a powerful force, a determination that will carry you through a huge variety of potential setbacks. Burning commitment is precisely the disappearance of self-doubt.

So here's the problem: In order to complete a book, you need an unmitigated, burning determination and passion, a deep certainty that you are on the right path, and an unswerving belief in yourself and your work. But if you don't have that kind of certainty and passion, you can't just go out and get it by an act of will. What can you do instead?

The answer, of course, is that there is a vast middle ground where most of us live, the area between the intention to do something and the burning determination that actually gets it done. I call it the 'fertile void'.

THE FERTILE VOID

With any creative act, there has to be a void first. A blank sheet of paper, an empty potter's wheel, a white canvas. There has to be a void inside the artist too, an empty space that eventually becomes filled with ideas, images or forms that were not there before.

The void is filled with tension. It may feel chaotic and diffuse. It may produce anxiety and confusion and the feeling of being overwhelmed. It is a moist, steamy environment in which self-doubts of all kinds happily take root and thrive.

But it is also the fertile ground in which brilliant creations are born. Out of chaos comes form and wholeness – if you have the patience and tenacity to move, gently but firmly, through the chaos.

I find that if I can remember three principles, I can always work my way through the fertile void to the creative process and the end product.

VIEW EVERYTHING YOU DO AS AN EXPERIMENT

The purpose of an experiment is to gather data, to learn something you didn't know before. The beauty of viewing everything you do as an experiment is that you can never fail. No matter what the outcome, you will have learned either what works or what doesn't work. Both are extremely valuable types of information.

Tallulah Bankhead said that if she had her life to live over again she would make all the same mistakes, only sooner.

There is no such thing as failure, only opportunity to learn, grow and renew your determination. Professional speaker Rosita Perez even goes so far as to say that every success is a missed opportunity to learn something new!

You will never regret sitting down and starting to write. What you may regret is being so unclear and uncertain (the fertile void), that you never experimented at all. As the nineteenth-century theologian Sören Kierkegaard put it, 'To dare is to lose one's footing temporarily; to not dare is to lose one's life.'

INSPIRATION COMES WHILE YOU ARE WORKING

I have already hit upon this theme several times in this book. There is no more important principle in creativity.

The only way to focus your passion, to discipline your muse, is to begin working. You must begin working, even if you have only the slightest idea of the direction in which you wish to move, because your work itself will be your greatest source of clarity and new ideas.

Again we are faced with our paradox: It is much more difficult to work and to produce anything lasting when you lack clarity and focus, when you are smack in the middle of the fertile void. Writing will feel like a struggle. But the only way out of the fertile void is to work. Your work itself will answer your questions and provide you with all your clarity and direction. Out of the process of working will come the brilliant ideas that will give your writing its signature quality.

Things take time. Perseverance is a combination of patience and persistence. Patience by itself will turn to lethargy or endless excuses. It may let you off the hook, but it will never get you to the joy of the creative flow. But persistence by itself can make you anxious and give a desperate quality to your work that robs you of the true pace of your

When you feel confident enough, select someone who is an experienced writer or even a professional editor or writing consultant and be prepared to learn what you can do to improve your work.

Writing is a two-person job. A good editor – or a person who is an expert in the field about which you are writing – will always see points that you have missed. Or such a person will analyse problems that you suspected were there but weren't sure enough – or became too lazy – to address, such as, 'This section is a bit repetitive,' or 'You need to expand this concept.' But it is a good idea to wait until you know you feel confident about what you have written before seeking this kind of thorough critique.

What if your reader's comments differ greatly from your opinion of what you wrote? Say you show it to a professional editor and she marks it all up and suggests you may be headed in the wrong direction?

This will be disappointing. But what you will do is consider her remarks and then decide whether you agree or disagree with them. If you decide you disagree, this will actually strengthen your inner certainty. In spite of negative comments, you still believe in your work. Or, maybe upon reflection, you will agree with much of what she said. Then you will be grateful to be working with a teacher who can help move you forward, and you will believe in your ability to improve.

The point is, what others think of your writing will help to shape your inner certainty and commitment, but in the end, you still know what you truly believe about your own work. Trust your own opinions. Cultivate your inner belief in your work. Learn to support – and criticise – your own work. In the end, you are the one who has to feel good about it. That's the whole point of writing.

It's perfectly okay to have self-doubts, fears and insecurities about your writing. What's not okay is to let them stop you. Only by working in spite of your self-doubts will you ever move beyond them, through the fertile void, to the sunny meadows where you are connected with your true passion and you know it. One day when you are immersed in your work, you will realise that your self-doubts are in the background somewhere, or that they have vanished altogether.

best creativity. It is the combination of patience and pers
will move you through the fertile void. Be gentle on your   e
begin. Begin now.   a

EXTERNAL VALIDATION CAN SUPPORT INNER CERTAINTY, BUT
CAN'T REPLACE IT

Most of us have been in that weird never-never land where w
written something we *think* we like – or maybe even know w
but we have no idea how it will be received by others.

Unless you are writing purely for your own pleasure, even
you have to show your work to someone.

Choose the time and the person or persons carefully.

Avoid the temptation to read something you just wrote to the
person who happens to phone you about something else. Inste
wait until you are certain that the piece is in a relatively finished sta
If you read a rough draft to someone, even if you say, 'But I'm goi
to clean it up and flesh it out,' the response you will receive is to th
rough draft you let the person see, not the potential finished produc

Choose someone whose opinion you respect, and deliberatel
choose someone who is likely to make supportive comment
someone who does not already have a tendency to be negativ
curmudgeonly or perfectionist.

Consider asking for the exact type of feedback you would a
would not like to hear. For example, 'I'm just looking for feedback
the content, the ideas. I want to know if you agree with this.' Or 'I ju
want to know whether I have made myself clear, whether this is ea
to follow and understand.' Or 'Please don't make any comme
about the grammar or style. I just want to know whether you like
approach I'm taking.'

If you are in the early stages of writing and have had virtually
feedback about your work, I strongly recommend that you ask y
listeners for positive comments only. For example, 'Please just tell
the parts that you especially like. I'm not ready for a full critique
but it would be helpful for me to hear what you do respond to.'

Enthusiastic positive response to your work can be a huge n
vator for you and a wonderful emotional boost. On the other ha
variety of miscellaneous opinions about what you might d
improve a certain piece will only confuse and probably disco
you. You are better off not even opening the door for this.

Procrastination

When I was six years old, so the family story goes, I asked my father, 'What does "procrastination" mean?'

'It means to put something off,' he told me.

That evening, he was driving a friend of mine home. In the car, I said to her, 'Be sure to tell my daddy where you want to be procrastinated.'

Since then, I have learned far more than I ever wanted to know about procrastination. I hope my methods for managing it will be useful to you too.

NAMING THE MONSTER

Most important, I believe that what most of us suffer, when we just can't seem to get started on a creative project that we very much want to do, is not procrastination at all, but rather 'acedia' (uh-see'-dee-uh). Let me explain.

Like many other people, I used to feel terrible on days when I knew I should be working but simply couldn't make myself get started. I would clear a day for writing weeks in advance, and then when the day arrived, somehow fritter it away. 'This is just procrastination,' I would tell myself. 'Don't give in to it. Break the job into tiny parts and do just one small task. Be disciplined. You can do this.'

Then one day, years ago now, a dear friend who is an artist and art teacher told me about acedia. Acedia, my friend explained, is the slow and arduous forward motion required to start a new project or to return to work after a break. Every creative person experiences acedia occasionally. It's a known, and completely acceptable, component of the creative process.

His words were magic for me. Suddenly, those awful hours – or days – when I thought I was ready to get started on a project but couldn't make anything happen were transformed for me. I wasn't lazy and undisciplined! Rather, I was allowing the creative forces inside me to gather steam. I was oiling the machinery, filling the tank with fuel, preparing for the journey. What a concept!

Procrastination is putting off something that you *don't* want to do – like writing an obligatory thank-you note, or cleaning out a cupboard. A lot of times, the world will go along just fine if the dreaded task gets put off so long that it finally drops off the 'to do' list altogether and never gets done at all.

Acedia is completely different from this. Acedia is the inner process you must go through in order to undertake a creative endeavour that you not only want to do but actually *long* to do. Such a creative task is often a huge undertaking. Say, for example, writing a book. Even if the endeavour itself isn't so huge, like writing a 700-word article, maybe what it represents for you in your life, your career, your self-image or your values feels immense. When you are working towards something that feels monumental, you may actually need *time* to work towards it. Relax, and view your delays as an integral part of the creative process.

Procrastination is resistance to doing a task. Acedia is the opposite: a slow, laborious giving-in to the task, a letting go of resistance, an embracing of the challenge of creativity.

Every time I take off in a plane, I play a game of trying to identify the exact moment when inertia (the tendency of a body at rest to remain at rest) has been overcome and the other inertia (the tendency of a body in motion to remain in motion) has set in. A staggering amount of energy is required to get that huge thing into motion.

This is exactly parallel to acedia. Acedia is the monumental effort required to overcome not being in motion, creatively speaking. Just like the plane, once you get into motion, the process will be almost effortless; it will sustain its own momentum. But you need to forgive yourself for experiencing difficulty in getting the huge creative machine started. Getting into motion requires far more energy and effort than staying in motion.

When my friend told me about acedia, I found it enormously comforting to hear what a common experience acedia is among artists of all flavours. My husband, Mayer, a ceramic artist who had been working in his own studio for some twenty years at the time, understood immediately when I explained it to him.

'It takes me six or eight weeks to create enough work for one firing in my large gas kiln,' he said. 'First I have to throw and alter and construct all the pieces. Then I have to glaze and decorate them.

Finally, I stack the kiln, fire it, and have the exciting experience of opening the cooled kiln to view my creations. But it is still not over. I have to photograph the work and ship it to galleries, place it in shows, or otherwise market and sell it.

'After I complete a cycle like that, the very idea of having to start it all over again, with nothing but bags of clay and an empty potter's wheel, seems overwhelming. It always takes me a while to work up to it. And the only process that ever works for me is to trick myself into working. I go into the studio. I tidy up in there. I organise my shelves, sweep the floors, order raw materials, tinker with the kiln, sketch ideas for pieces, and then one day, when I'm not quite watching, I find I'm seated at my wheel creating work again – and absolutely thrilled to be doing so. Once I'm immersed in my work again, it flows and I feel the joy of creativity.'

Of course, understanding and accepting acedia does not make it any more pleasant to endure. Acedia is usually painful; in fact, it can be excruciatingly so. But when you name it appropriately and see it for what it is, then, instead of hating and belittling yourself for these painful times, you can instead treat yourself gently and lovingly, as though you have a mild illness and just need to take it easy for a few days. This is a distinction that makes an enormous difference – in both the quality of your acedia and the duration of it.

Even though I have been spreading the word about acedia for years, I still never anticipate it. When I am preparing to start writing after a break, I'm usually excited and eager to get to work. I may even get as far as sitting in front of my computer. But then, mysteriously, I become very sleepy and find I must lie down for a short nap. Or I think of several phone calls that seem ever so urgent. I convince myself I can't start on a creative project until I've cleared my desk. I become obsessed with working out how to make my computer do some wonderful new trick I have managed quite well without all these years. Or, worst of all, I start surfing the Net or spending hours on useless e-mail correspondence.

As we said, these hours – or even days – can be most unpleasant. As my friends know, I can become quite anxious during bouts of acedia – even though I understand what is happening and fully believe I will get through it. Once, just when I was really going to get started that day, the hard disk on my computer crashed. My resistance to beginning was so huge, I managed to get my computer to conspire with me!

But my understanding of acedia has transformed it for me. I know from much experience that being angry and tough with myself, and forcing myself to work, simply won't be effective. The more I resist and fight my torpor, the more it will persist. Instead, I give in to it. I have lived with it long enough to know that it won't last forever. I choose to believe that something important is happening inside me, that my brain is cranking itself up, my muse is dusting herself off. So I let go and trust a course of events over which I, for the moment, have no control.

Sometimes, when I realise I am having an acedia attack and I just *know* that nothing worthwhile is going to get written that day no matter how I try to force it, I deliberately pamper myself. Other times, I throw myself into the errands, letters, phone calls and organising that seem so much more urgent than my writing. Often, I can actually accomplish quite a bit during my acedia attacks. I also notice that, during my acedia days, I am *thinking about* what I will write, so that when I finally do get round to it, I already know exactly how I will start or organise my material – which can make the actual onset of writing much easier.

After I have given in to acedia a few times, like Mayer, I gently trick myself into moving through it. I type gibberish or challenge myself to write only one sentence, or I write a letter to my muse. Inevitably, once the words start coming, I find myself back in the 'flow', like a jet easily cruising through the air. Before long, the creative cruise becomes exhilarating and well worth the massive effort that was required to get it going.

The secret, then, to moving through acedia is twofold:

1. Keep a loving attitude toward your acedia, even though it may be painful. Be gentle with yourself. Accept that you are in a difficult phase of the creative process, and don't fight it. Often, the more anguished the acedia, the more exciting the creative product when it finally does emerge.

2. Trick yourself into *somehow* getting started. Staying with your creative endeavour is much easier than getting it off the ground, once you can get the momentum started.

Let's now look in a little more detail at step two.

GETTING-STARTED STRATEGIES

Any of the old stand-by remedies for 'procrastination' can be quite useful for tricking yourself into getting started. For example:

- Divide your task into small, manageable steps and focus on *only one* of those steps.
- Agree with yourself that you will work on your task for only five minutes – that's all.
- Do something related but easier. For example, type nonsense or stream of consciousness.
- Write a letter to your muse about what you long for, or about the nature of your resistance to getting started.
- Organise your work space. Set up your computer. 'Sharpen your pencils'.
- Start writing, not at the beginning of your project, but smack in the middle somewhere, a place where you already have a good idea what you are going to write.

Your acedia with regard to any creative project will be greatly exacerbated if you genuinely have no idea how to get started or exactly what to do first. Whenever that is true, then the very first thing you must do is define a limited, manageable first step. If you are a 'right brain' type for whom organising a project into linear steps is close to impossible, consider enlisting the help of a friend who has a reputation for being well-organised. Plan an hour together. You talk about what you want to accomplish, what you want your finished product to look like. Let your friend help you make a list of small steps in a logical order.

ON WAITING UNTIL YOU ARE READY

Just as there is never a perfect time to have a baby, there is never a perfect time to write a book.

It is perfectly okay to begin a creative project before you know what the completed result will be. Writer Wendy Lichtman often talks with children about creative writing. She told me they are always amazed to learn that, when she begins a piece, she may have no idea how it will end. They assume a writer has a full-blown idea and that writing it out is more like being a typist.

It's not that way. Inspiration comes while you are working. Writing is a process not of recording what you want to say but of discovering what you want to say.

So don't wait forever for the right time or until you have enough information. Your main job as a writer is to *get started*.

Envy

There will always be someone who is more successful than you. However you define success for yourself, whatever your most cherished goals are, someone will get there first, or will somehow achieve more of exactly what you want.

When this happens, it is normal and even appropriate to feel angry, threatened, discouraged, jealous, betrayed by the universe – any number of emotions that I have grouped loosely together under the term 'envy'.

When you compare yourself to a writer who is doing well or whose work you admire, self-doubts can easily well up in you: 'I'll never be able to write that well, or be that successful.' 'How can it take him only six months to write a book when it takes me six years?' 'How come she can write for eight hours a day, and I can only write for two?' 'Why is it so easy for her to sell her stuff, when I can't even get my project off the ground?'

There may be people who are sufficiently confident about their own work or who are so spiritually evolved that nothing ever upsets their inner balance. But for most of the writers I know, occasional attacks of envy are inescapable.

Over the years, I've developed strategies for taming the green-eyed monster. I hope some of my remedies will be helpful for you as well.

ACCEPT IT

Like any creative activity, writing is extremely personal. Your writing is unique. You labour intensely to produce an article or a chapter. When you're 'on', you know deep inside that your work is really good. Naturally, you would love to be recognised for your talent. You want others to be moved by what you write, to find it *unusually* helpful, provocative, entertaining, informative, clever, beautiful or innovative. When someone else receives the recognition you crave, of course you are going to have at least a twinge, and maybe a full-blown pang, of jealousy.

If you pretend to ignore this pang, or you actively fight it off, telling yourself you should be more mature, that you shouldn't allow these things to get to you, your symptoms will get worse. Now, you not only feel envy; in addition, you feel angry with yourself for feeling envy.

Instead of whirling into this downward spiral, indulge your envious feelings – for a little while. Forgive yourself for being less than perfect. Feel your envy fully. Actually pay attention to it. As we've observed, envy is a stew of emotions. Which ones are you feeling most keenly? What particular incident triggered your envy this time? Exactly what does this person have that you want?

One possibility is to exaggerate the feeling, to give the emotion that is building up in you an outlet, a 'discharge'. Throw a little fit, or write a 'letter to the editor' (that you will of course *never* send!). Figuratively burn this person in effigy: 'His or her writing isn't a tenth as good as mine anyway. The whole thing of who sells to publishers, who gets on the bestseller list, is all rigged to start with. People with talent but no connections don't have a chance.' I can't have your fit for you, but you get the idea. You don't have to be charitable or nice. You don't have to be 'spiritually evolved'. Just express your raw emotions – in private.

A second possibility is, instead of exaggerating your feelings, simply be aware of them. Actually notice exactly what is going on inside you, as though you were an outside observer.

If you like, sit quietly, close your eyes, breathe easily, and let yourself focus completely on these feelings. This might be revealing for you and offer you surprising insights. You may find that the feelings diminish in the same way a wispy cloud will often disappear if you gaze at it in a focused way for a few minutes.

My own rule is, I'm allowed to be angry or upset for thirty minutes – if I need that long. If my envy is just a little twinge, five minutes may be enough. Then, I move on to step two.

TAKE A GIFT FROM YOUR ENVY BEFORE YOU LEAVE IT

The perfect antidote to envy is not, as you may suspect, success. As we know, so often those who are most 'successful' in one area of their lives admit to painful deficits in other areas. No, the perfect antidote to envy is self-love. When you know deep inside that you are on absolutely the right path for yourself, or you are in the process of uncovering what that path is, and you are doing the best you can right now given all the external and internal parameters, another person's achievement will not throw you off centre.

Of course developing self-love and self-confidence is an ongoing task for all of us. It involves accepting the parts of ourselves that we *don't* like so that we won't have to keep hiding from ourselves but can love our whole, real selves. That's why an episode of envy can be a powerful tool when put to use in the service of developing self-love.

So examine your envy to see what you can learn from it. You might ask, what does this envy tell me about my own goals? What does it tell me about my inner strength? What can I change in my life so that I can achieve the goals I want faster? In what specific ways can I allow this envy to motivate me? Is there anything specific this person did to achieve this goal that I could also do? What does this envy show me that I don't like about myself? (This question may be somewhat painful, but remember, with personal growth as with physical exercise, if understood properly, pain often leads to gain.)

REPLACE THE UNPLEASANT THOUGHTS WITH PLEASANT ONES

You can't make yourself *not* think about something; by trying not to think about it, you are thinking about it.

What works beautifully instead is to think about something else quite deliberately. The mind has room for only one thought at a time. If you put a nice one in there, the ugly ones will automatically get crowded out.

Think about all that you have accomplished. Instead of comparing yourself to the person who triggered your envy, compare yourself to your own personal best. You are on your very own private journey that no one else can take for you. And you are doing the best you can. That's absolutely all you can ask of yourself. Someone else's getting a lucky break or achieving a goal before you did does not diminish your achievements in the slightest.

If you were someone else looking at your life, what would you envy in you? Fill your mind with those warm, pleasant, energising thoughts.

Focus deliberately on your own writing project. Spend some time reading what you have already written and savour the pleasure of your own work. Plan exactly what you will do next, and when you will do it.

Find a thought that gives you an enormous amount of pleasure. It might be something you have accomplished or are about to accomplish, a passage you have written, someone's enthusiastic response to something you have written, a skill or talent that you possess that you feel good about. Now, whenever this envy thing enters your brain, swiftly and deliberately start thinking your pleasurable thoughts. The more you practice this, and the more you see how well it works, the easier it will become. Pretty soon, you'll find that you have forgotten about the unpleasant thoughts, or that when they do arise, the pain is hardly noticeable; you have moved beyond it.

Realise two things: First, you have control over what you choose to think about. And second, comparison is the basis of all misery. The process of comparing yourself to others in order to see who is better is toxic whether you come out on the top or the bottom. If you compare yourself with people who are more successful, you will feel discouraged. But if you compare yourself to people who are less successful than you, you will be belittling them in order to feel better about yourself. In the long run, that doesn't feel good either. It weakens you. It tells you that you are dependent upon someone else's shortcomings to feel good about yourself. And it robs you of the opportunity to develop an inner strength and confidence that is far more solid and that can support other people as well as yourself.

Like an addiction, comparison may be a hard habit to break. But in the end, the most self-nurturing path you can take is to refrain from doing it.

AVOID TOXIC PEOPLE AND
SURROUND YOURSELF WITH SUPPORT

There are two kinds of people in the world: angels and balloon poppers.

Angels have helium balloons tied to their shoulders and arms, so that they always hover just above the ground. They go about helping other people to feel good about themselves and offering help and support wherever they can. Of course they receive lots of support and love in return, which fills their balloons with more helium and keeps them floating happily about.

Balloon poppers are anxious and insecure. They can't stand

seeing angels having so much fun. So they go about with needles, popping balloons, sometimes obviously, sometimes ever so subtly. Sometimes, they can even cause angels to fall to the ground.

We all start out as angels, with happy dispositions and a willing spirit. Our balloons are filled with hope, excitement, good will, generosity and self-love.

But balloon poppers are everywhere. With their little insults, their self-centredness, their self-importance, their fears and insecurities, their big egos and their greed, they go about destroying everyone else's balloons and gathering more people into the ranks of the balloon poppers.

The secret to success in this world and the best way to avoid envy altogether is to *stay away from balloon poppers and spend lots of time with angels.*

Curiously, most of us don't do this. Children, for whom angels are most important and balloon poppers most destructive, unfortunately have no choice. But as adults who do have choice, we are often inexplicably drawn to toxic, unsupportive people.

One particular type of balloon popper is more likely to evoke envy in you than any other kind: narcissists. A few always seem to be lurking about writers' conferences freely wielding their needles. Causing other people to feel envious of them is actually intrinsic to the way narcissists behave, so when you are around one whose strategy is working, you can feel lousy. Let me explain.

Where most of us have an inner sense of self, narcissists have a big hole. To replace this missing identity, narcissists pour all their energy into building up a strong image to present to the world. Since the only way they can *feel* okay is to *appear* okay to the rest of the world, they are highly motivated to achieve the outer trappings of success, and to display them freely. Narcissists tend to be focused upon themselves and are not the kind of people who become truly invested in another person's success or happiness.

After you have been around a narcissist, you may find that you suddenly feel sad, discouraged, hopeless or small. Extreme narcissists can make you feel as if even your very goals are petty and worthless. The only really fun, exciting, worthwhile life is the one the narcissist is lucky enough to be leading.

What happened is that you became an unwitting pawn in someone else's effort to stay on a self-made pedestal that is essential to his or her well-being.

You can't change narcissists, and you can't change your relationship with them. When you encounter someone like this who seems to evoke envy in you, try to have as little contact with that person as possible. Recognise a toxic relationship for what it is, and get out of it.

It feels very, very different to be with an angel. Angels compliment and praise your work. They are genuinely interested in you. They listen to you and ask you questions about you and your work. They freely share their own insecurities, self-doubts and failures because they realise that is one way human beings connect with each other, and they are interested in connection, trust, genuine friendship and caring. After you leave the presence of an angel, you feel buoyed up, excited, encouraged, energised.

Of course I have exaggerated these two types to make a point. In the real world, most people are not pure types but a mixture. We all have some helium in our balloons, more on some days than on others. And we all hide a few needles away in our pockets too.

My main point is this: When, after direct or indirect contact with a person, you feel deflated, don't stop to analyse why or justify it. Don't be lured by the person's glitter. Don't put yourself down. *Just make it a point to avoid that person in the future.* For however complex the combination of circumstances, some situations are just plain toxic. There may be little you can do to alter that. So do whatever you need to do to avoid them.

In addition, actively search out people who leave you feeling excited, energised and encouraged. One of the best ways to do this is to focus on providing that feeling for other people whenever you have a chance. When you read something you like, make a point of seeking out the author and saying so. Offer compliments freely to others. Write little notes of appreciation to people who do you favours or whom you enjoyed meeting or whose writing you like. You know yourself how good it feels when someone singles out one particular idea, metaphor or paragraph you wrote for special comment. If people don't tell you what they respond most to, you'll never know. So provide that boost for other people. I haven't met a person yet who said, 'I've been receiving too many nice comments lately.' In fact, the most direct route to feeling good about *yourself* is a genuine, loving connection with another human being.

As writers, we are in luck. We have a good supply of angels in our ranks, eager to form writers' circles and to exchange work and mutual support. Which brings me to my fourth strategy.

JOIN OR FORM 'HELIUM' CIRCLES OR PARTNERSHIPS

You can actually structure your 'writing buddy' relationships so that you maximise mutual support and virtually eliminate balloon popping. Whether you exchange writing with just one other person or with a group that meets regularly, make a rule that you will give each other only positive, supportive feedback – only helium, no needles.

There is of course a time and place to ask for editorial help and concrete suggestions for improvement. Select your writing mentors carefully. Ask for corrective feedback only from people who are experienced and whose opinion you have reason to trust, and only at a time when you are prepared to hear what a consultant or editor has to say. Always remember that receiving feedback about how you can improve will be far easier and more effective if you have received lots of helium already, if you have a strong sense of what you and other people really like about your writing.

Author and public speaking consultant Lee Glickstein developed a method for coaching speakers that grew in popularity so quickly it has now become a nationwide phenomenon in the States. He calls his model Speaking Circles. It is common for professional speakers to become emotional when they talk about how quickly and magically Speaking Circles enhanced their confidence and accelerated their careers.

Lee's idea is simple: Members of a Speaking Circle each speak, first for three minutes, and then, in a second round, for five. Their main focus is to establish rapport and connection with their listeners. After each 'speech', every listener reports only what he or she most liked about the short presentation.

As Lee and many speakers have found, positive support is a magic elixir. It can motivate and inspire you to a greatness that all the 'criticism' in the world can never accomplish. If you don't believe in yourself, you'll never try. And when you do believe in yourself, nothing can stop you. Belief in yourself is ultimately an inner experience, but external support can bring it into being and keep it alive and well.

I believe writers would do well to adapt the Speaking Circle model and to create 'Helium Circles'.

What is a Helium Circle?

It consists of five to ten people who are at approximately the same stage of their writing. They can be a mix of fiction and non-fiction writers, as long as each category is represented by at least two people. The group can meet weekly, bi-weekly, or monthly, but all members should agree to attend every time if they are well and in town.

The circle can choose a facilitator or might want to rotate the job. The facilitator should remind the group of the ground rules and watch the clock so that everyone gets a turn.

The ground rules are simple. Each member reads something that he or she has written for a pre-determined length of time, say five or ten minutes. Then, all group members respond to the reading by saying what they like about it in general and identifying two or three portions, ideas, metaphors, words, sentences or paragraphs that they responded to in a positive way.

Then, the next person reads.

But what if you do have critical feedback that you just know would be helpful to the reader, and you are dying to share it? The anecdote about the teacher doesn't illustrate the point. The beginning is too wordy. The most important point was buried. The third point should go first.

Make notes for yourself if you like. But don't share this information. Realise three things: (1) You may feel strongly about your suggestions, but they are only your opinion. Other group members may disagree with you and will have other suggestions. A group of people should never attempt to edit a piece of writing. (2) If this person is serious about writing, he or she will seek out suggestions for improvement and receive criticism at the appropriate time and place. If you want to volunteer to mentor the person and you have the time and interest, offer to meet individually with him or her later. (3) Hearing what *does work* is valuable feedback for the writer, as it will be for you when it is your turn. The point of the group is to leave everyone feeling buoyed up and ready to write more.

Some evenings, your group may decide to discuss a particular topic, like when and where you write, how you edit your own work, what you have learned about various agents, or dozens of other topics of interest to you all.

HELIUM PARTNERS

A variation on a Helium Circle that meets in person is a smaller group or partnership in which you exchange writing by fax, e-mail or post.

One woman told me she and a writing buddy exchange an essay every two weeks. Their agreement when they receive the other person's essay is to highlight the parts they like, write one small suggestion or idea at the bottom and promptly return the piece. She said the system keeps her writing and that the positive feedback is a joy to receive every two weeks.

Consider finding yourself a helium buddy or buddies, and become each other's writing angels.

I can't emphasise enough the importance of consistent positive feedback about your work, no matter what level you have or haven't achieved. Even if your beginning efforts are mediocre, hearing others say what they do like about it will keep you working, and only by working will you improve. And no matter how much recognition you have received for your writing, there is still no pleasure quite like hearing that you have somehow connected with one more person.

We all thrive on positive feedback about our work. One way to be sure you get yours is to structure it into your relationships with other writers. I highly recommend it.

* * *

To summarise then, envy and comparisons that discourage you are facts of life. When you are seized by an attack of envy, first, accept yourself as normal. Experience the envy, and see what you can learn from it.

Realise that you are on your own unique path and that any comparison with another person serves only to deter you from your goal. To relieve the envy or unpleasant comparison, concentrate on pleasurable, encouraging thoughts about yourself and your own work. Congratulate yourself for what you have accomplished. Envision your own goals. Realise that they are private and personal, and assure yourself that your schedule for achieving them is perfectly fine. Focus on the positive parts of your creative life, and be patient with yourself.

Above all, avoid contact with people who trigger bad feelings in you, for whatever reason. Cultivate relationships with people whom you find to be supportive and energising. And *deliberately* build positive support for your creative work into your life.

Reaping the Joy

During the six years I was writing my first book, and blundering through all the wrong approaches to getting published, I had one persistent fantasy: After my book came out, I would be seated at the dining room table at Esalen Institute in Big Sur, a conference centre famous for its personal growth workshops. Someone at the table would say, 'And what do you do, Susan?' I would say, 'I'm a writer. I've just published my first book called, *If I'm So Wonderful, Why Am I Still Single?*' Then several people at the table would gasp and exclaim, 'You wrote that book? I *love* that book. It changed my life!'

Over time, I did receive numerous letters from grateful readers. But this particular little episode never happened. For years, the only response I ever received was, 'Oh, that sounds interesting!' or 'Gosh, I think I need that book!'

Once, in Cleveland, I was the guest on their popular morning TV chat show, after which I signed books at a table in a crowded shopping mall – wearing the same clothes. I thought surely someone would come over and say, 'Weren't you on *Morning Exchange* this morning? You were a wonderful guest!' Not a soul recognised me.

About four years later, when my second book was published, an Australian publisher bought it and flew me over there for a media tour. (This was one of the loveliest perks my writing has earned me.) I was having breakfast in a small hotel dining room where only one other couple was seated. Naturally, we struck up a conversation. I got around to telling them I write books about relationships.

'Oh, are you a psychologist?' the woman asked.

'No, actually my background is in the ministry,' I told her.

'Really?' she responded. 'Some of the best psychology books are written by ministers. Scott Peck was a minister, you know. I teach classes for singles in Perth, and there is one book I use more than any other, and it is by a woman who is a minister. This is the most useful book I've ever seen on the subject. I insist that all my students read it, and we use so many of the exercises from it. It's called, *If I'm So*

Wonderful, Why Am I Still Single? The writing is just so clear, and this woman covers every question singles have. There is one part – '

I was getting embarrassed, and finally decided I'd better interrupt and let her know who I was. I sort of smiled and pointed to myself.

'What? You're Susan Page? I can't believe it!'

Her reaction made up for all the anonymity I had endured for five years. It was quite a special moment – for both of us. After we got over our shock, we couldn't stop laughing.

Most writers have stories like this, moments when they can experience the impact that their writing has had on the life of another person. These moments are very precious to us as writers, because as we are writing, we have no idea whether what we say and the way we say it is going to connect with readers.

Writer Winnie Shows received a most unusual thank-you for a piece she wrote for the *Los Angeles Times*.

> Near the Hollywood Freeway, there was a wonderful mural of an old woman with a colourful afghan around her by a muralist named Twitchell. In my article, I said that it reminded me of my grandmother's afghan. My aunt sent a copy of the article to a long-time friend of my grandmother, who had died ten years earlier, and the woman was so moved, she made me an afghan like the one in the mural. I also received a postcard from the woman who had posed for the mural. It was a high point in my writing career.

Susan Luke was selling her book, *Log Cabin Logic: Creating Success Where You Are with What You Have,* in the back of the room at her own presentations, and, though she had arranged for distribution in local bookshops, she didn't really expect to see it there. One Saturday afternoon, browsing at a local bookshop, she saw it!

'I was almost hyperventilating, I was so excited. There I was, dressed in T-shirt and shorts, looking less than stunning, when I suddenly found myself grabbing perfect strangers and showing them my book. When they looked at me like I was crazy, I turned to the back cover and pointed dramatically to my photo, stating the obvious, "See? See? This is me on a good hair day!" '

To touch the heart of any reader is a joy. But perhaps the joy is even more special when that person is a child. Cynthia Chin-Lee told me this story:

A teacher shared this incident with me. She had read aloud my children's book, *Almond Cookies and Dragon Well Tea*, a multicultural book of friendship and sharing. One of her students had not spoken in class at all. His mother had died, and he was still grieving. My book includes a family altar where the main character, Nancy, remembers her deceased great-grandfather. When this little boy heard about Nancy, he began to talk about his mother and how he wished to remember her.

When writers are asked to tell about the joys of writing, what they think about first, I've found, is the joy of the *results* of their writing. But do actors act only so they can be recognised for three minutes at the Academy Awards? No, they act because they love to act. I believe the same thing is true for writers, though they talk about it less. The real reason we love knowing that our writing has touched others in some way, has been successful, is that . . . it means we can keep on writing.

When I am in the middle of a project, what I want most in the world is a whole day with no appointments or interruptions, so I can write. I love the feeling of waking up and knowing that nothing else besides throwing on some clothes and grabbing some breakfast stands in the way of getting back to my computer. I love the experience of looking at the clock and discovering it has been four or even six hours since I looked at it the last time. The exhilaration of reading something I just wrote and feeling really good about it is as exciting to me as, well . . . sex! When I write, I feel I am doing the work that I was meant to do on this planet. And I am deeply, palpably grateful (a) that I discovered this work, having been off in another direction for my first forty years, and (b) that my work has been successful enough to allow me to keep on doing it. Sometimes, at the end of a day of writing, I feel so energised and happy, I actually dance around my house.

I have difficult writing days too, of course, usually when I can't figure out how to organise a set of ideas, or I'm not sure quite what I want to say, so I have to experiment, and the experiments don't work. Or I try to express an idea and just don't feel satisfied with it. But I once climbed an eighty-foot perpendicular rock wall under the guidance of my wilderness-instructor son. I remember thinking at moments that it was the hardest thing I had ever done in my life, that I just couldn't make my body do this. And I felt mentally challenged:

There was just *no way* past a certain spot. But I remember shouting with joy when I actually reached the top. I was elated!

It's the same kind of joy I experience when I finally get through a stuck place in my writing.

What is joy?

It has something to do with setting challenges and meeting them. It has something to do with connecting with other people. And it has something to do with being able to find and express your unique self.

As we've seen, writing involves all three of these. Let's talk about the last one for a moment.

The aspects of yourself that set you apart from everyone else in the world are extremely precious. Writing gives you the opportunity to access your unique self, and to express it. That is a big part of why it can be such a deeply joyful experience.

We live in a world that systematically suppresses individuality. Most people spend their lives doing someone else's work, not their own. If our highest spiritual calling is to be as fully ourselves as we can be, then, as a poster I once saw put it, 'From God's point of view, most of us are unemployed.'

As a writer, you are expressing your singular, remarkable self. Even if the subject matter is identical to someone else's, no one else will write the same book you will write. No one else has the same story to tell or the same way of telling it. Your writing is a unique contribution to the planet. Your only job is to write to the very best of your ability, and to keep stretching and learning so that you are always expanding your creative capacity.

To reiterate then, certainly there is joy when you find that you connect with other people, that your creative expression in some way enriches their lives. But never become so focused on this goal that you miss the excitement of the *process* of writing, or of any creative expression.

In his study of optimal experience which he calls *Flow*, psychologist Mihaly Csikszentmihalyi says, 'It is by being fully involved with every detail of our lives . . . that we find happiness,' by 'achieving control over the contents of our consciousness.'

Others talk about experiencing true joy in their creative efforts when they feel most in alignment with who they truly are and with the universe about them. Ceramic artist Neil Tetkowski told me, 'I produce my best work when I am harmonising with the things that are bigger than I am.'

Of course, there may be many of you reading this who have published or hope to publish a book, for whom writing is not your first passion at all. The kind of joy we have been talking about here comes to you from speaking in front of a group, or teaching children, or gardening, or caring for animals, or closing a business deal. For you, writing may simply be a means to some other end. You can translate the same things we have said about writing to your life's passion.

But if writing is your passion, whatever monsters you have to tame to get yourself writing and to guide your project until it sees the light of publication, tame them. This is your chance to feel the exhilaration of creative expression. You have the opportunity both to express your unique message and to connect with other people in a way that can make a genuine difference to their lives. Set a challenge for yourself, relish every good hour or day of writing, celebrate every little victory, and then feel the rush of joy when you are actually holding your very own book in your hand – along with letters from grateful readers.

I sincerely hope this book serves as a lantern that brightens your journey through the writing meadow and the publishing labyrinth, and makes it pleasant, easy, fast and successful.

LET'S KEEP TALKING!

I was motivated to write this book because I found much of the information in it virtually impossible to find. I hope that by collecting hundreds of tidbits in one place, I have been able to spare you some of the hard knocks that I have endured while learning them.

But I don't want the intense conversations to end! If you have something to add, please write or e-mail. Since there will no doubt be revisions of this book, I'm especially interested in any anecdote in which you show that a particular suggestion proved to be either useful or wrong. What did you need to know that turned out to be nowhere in this book? And especially, what have you learned from your own experience that would be helpful to other writers? I will, of course, credit you with any advice you offer that makes it into the next revision, and I'll do my best to respond to you directly.

Write to me at Shortest Distance Dialogues, 1941 Oregon Street, Berkeley, California 94703, USA, or e-mail me at Authortalk@aol.com.

See you at the bookshop!

Sample Proposal

I have included here one complete non-fiction proposal. It is often most helpful to see an actual proposal when you are working on your own.

The sample non-fiction proposal I've chosen is the actual proposal I used to sell this book. Except for disguising the authors and titles I used in my comparative section, I have not changed one word. I thought it would be useful for you to see how the proposal compares to the finished book.

The first thing you will notice is that the actual book differs quite a bit from what I thought I would write when I was putting together the proposal. This will virtually always be true. The writing process stimulates new ideas and suggests alternative ways to organise material that you can never anticipate before you begin to work. Several of my Steps changed as I wrote because the material fell more tidily into different categories from those I had first imagined. Note also that I originally envisaged Part II as a series of 'laws for publishing success'. But as I got into the writing, I realised that scheme was flat and that what might work much better would be to organise my suggestions according to the problems that writers often experience. I tried that and was much happier with it. If your final book 'works', and if it delivers the spirit of what you proposed in your proposal, no one is going to hold you to exactly what you thought you might write when you first started organising your book idea.

Here then, is the actual proposal for this book. I hope it will answer many of your questions as you write your own.

How to Get Published and Make a Lot of Money

A Book Proposal

by
Susan Page

1941 Oregon Street
Berkeley, CA 94703
Fax: 510/xxx-xxxx
Phone: 510/xxx-xxxx

A Book Proposal for
How to Get Published
and Make a Lot of Money

Proposal Table of Contents

Overview

To aspiring writers, getting a book published can seem like an un-fathomable mystery. What's worse, guidebooks currently available on the subject only intimidate them further. Straightforward answers to simple questions like, 'Why should I use an agent?' remain elusive in the current literature where an aspiring writer can get a course on the publishing industry but never be told exactly what constitutes a winning proposal, why agents are useful or how to get endorsements.

In this pithy book, Susan Page finally tells writers exactly what they need to know to get published – and that's all. Her book is thorough, but precise.

Much of Susan Page's advice to other writers is completely original. Her twenty discrete, chronological steps organise the writer's experience as never before. While other books offer vague pros and cons on the use of agents, Page makes a strong case for using an agent, and explains exactly how to select and acquire one. Page replaces the dread 'procrastination' with a new concept, 'acedia' (spiritual sloth or the inability to get back to work after a break), and explains that it is a necessary part of the creative process. She includes a thorough discussion of titles and shows writers how to find a good one. She introduces writers to the Mastermind, an indispensable tool for authors.

This book is a breakthrough because Susan Page is not an agent or editor giving advice to writers, but another writer. She understands the feelings and the inner struggles of writing and trying to get published. In the inimitable manner readers so love in her other books, she provides effective encouragement and advice at each phase of the process.

Susan acquired her expertise by, as she puts it, 'wandering in the publishing desert for six years' before she sold her first book. She has since published two books very successfully, and now that she has figured out how to do it, she doesn't see any reason to keep what works a secret. She has tested the material in this book in workshops for three years, has assisted more than a dozen authors who actually sold their proposals, and helped one writer increase her advance by $50,000.

In Susan Page's previous books, she transformed what were widely believed to be virtually impossible experiences – finding a mate and sustaining a thriving marriage – into pleasant, manageable, even exciting tasks. Here, she works her magic again with the allegedly formidable task of getting published. Writers discouraged by massive tomes with chapters like 'Recovering the Rights to Your Out-of-Print Book' will read Susan Page's book with a smile and a huge sigh of relief – and then turn around and get to work.

Market for the Book

Pat Smith's *Guide to Getting Published* has sold 250,000 copies in seven years. That's almost 36,000 books a year for seven years! Books on how to get published sell consistently because there are always new people moving into the writing phase of their lives.

This book is destined to replace Smith's classic because it will be shorter and more approachable; organised in an appealing, user-friendly way; and vastly more thorough in the areas in which first-time authors really need help. It will omit descriptions of the publishing industry that are so intimidating (and unnecessary) for first-time writers.

But this book will go far beyond Smith's book, because it is designed to encourage people who have only the vaguest writing aspirations.

More people are turning to writing now than ever before as a result of corporate downsizing, the continuing rise of entrepreneurs who want to write about their unique experience, and the ever-growing increase in specialised information. The huge population of people who 'want to write a book some day' who leaf through fat, complex publishing guides and put them back on the shelf, discouraged, will *buy* this book because it is *encouraging* and tells the hopeful writer exactly how to take the first step.

The circulation of *Writer's Digest* magazine is 247,640; their readership is 450,000. According to their own surveys, 50 per cent of their readers are attempting to make their first sale. Using the most conservative figures, that's 123,820 people who need this book right now.

At least 10,000 people attend the over 200 writers' conferences held across the nation annually, and, according to Shaw's *Guide to Writers Conferences,* most of them have never attended such a conference before. That's 10,000 *new* writers per year.

How to Get Published will be purchased by the 250,000 people whose copy of Smith's guide is still gathering dust *plus* at least 36,000 new writers every year. This won't just be a backlist book; it will be a *big* backlist book – for many years.

The Author

Susan Page is the author of *If I'm So Wonderful, Why Am I Still Single?,* published in hardcover by Viking in 1988 and later in paperback by Bantam, and *Now That I'm Married, Why Isn't Everything Perfect?* published in 1993 by Little, Brown. It took her six years to sell her first book, largely because of terrible advice she received from apparently knowledgeable people and books.

Since she connected with the *right* people and learned how straightforward getting published can be, Susan began to assist others with their efforts to get published. In 1990, she presented a workshop for the National Convention of the National Speakers' Association entitled 'How to Earn $100,000 for your First Non-fiction Book.' The workshop was so well-received that the audio tape of it became one of NSA's most requested cassettes. She has since assisted more than a dozen authors who actually sold their proposals under her guidance, and helped one writer increase her advance by $50,000.

Susan Page's own two books have received widespread critical acclaim *(Kirkus:* 'Behold a wonder! A self-help book that is intelligent, upbeat, practical, useful, winning and even wise. . . . First-rate of its kind.'). They have been translated into fourteen foreign languages between them and have been excerpted in *Cosmopolitan, Glamour, McCalls, Self, New Woman* and *Woman* magazines. Susan's national media appearances include *Good Morning America, Oprah* (three times), *Geraldo, Sonya Live,* CNN's *News Night Update* and National Public Radio.

Susan is a graduate of Oberlin College and San Francisco Theological Seminary. She began her career as a Protestant campus minister, was the executive director of a large domestic abuse prevention agency, and is the former Director of Women's Programmes at the University of California, Berkeley. She is now a full-time writer and speaker.

Analysis of the Competition

[Authors, titles, publishers and dates have been changed to protect the innocent.]

Guide to Getting Published by Pat Smith
Fancy New York Publishers, New York 1986

Smith is a rambler. Readers who are patient and themselves well-organised may eventually figure out what they need to do, but not without wading through superfluous and confusing information about the entire publishing world. *How to Get Published* is a tightly-organised, step-by-step guide.

In addition, Smith focuses on the publishing industry, while *How to Get Published* focuses on the aspiring writer, what he or she needs to know, when to do what, how to handle specific classic situations, and even what feelings to anticipate.

Another Guide to Getting Published by Pat Smith, Jr.
How-To-Write Publishers, Denver 1982

When Smith's book discusses book proposals, it lures the unsuspecting writer into a project much more massive than a book proposal ever needs to be. It even asks writers to mention how much they spent to get the proposal typed! I have seen several Smith-guided proposals that were entire loose-leaf notebooks of more than two hundred pages. Writers who come to me having read this book feel oppressed by the weight of the task they face. By contrast, *How to Get Published* breaks the project down into precise, achievable steps that excite readers and leave them feeling inspired and ready to work.

Yet Another Guide to Getting Published by Pat Smith II
ABC Publishers, New York 1986

Smith's book is also chatty and randomly organised. It preys upon potential writers' negative stereotypes of the publishing process with chapter titles like 'Publishing Horror Stories' and 'When Your Editor Quits on You'. With few subtitles throughout the weighty text, the book would be difficult to use as a reference when looking for the answer to a particular question. It contains good information for someone interested in a career in the publishing industry, but it is not even designed as a precise guide for the first-time writer, as is *How to Get Published.*

Information Useful to Authors by Pat Smith III
Overkill Publishers, New York 1991

Smith has made a useful contribution by providing far more information about some publishing houses and agents than can be found in other reference books. This book includes essays in the back of the book on proposal writing, ghostwriters, etc. A useful reference book but not a systematic guide.

How to Succeed in Publishing by Pat Smith IV
Getting Better Publishers, New York 1988

Almost 400 pages of in-depth information of interest to the publishing professional – but far beyond what the first-time author needs or cares about. This might be an interesting book for an author to read between the submission of the final manuscript and the publication date. By contrast, *How to Get Published* is a chronologically organised guide for the first-time author.

Note: None of the above books is written by a writer from the writer's point of view. All of these authors are publishing professionals. The writer's perspective is different and needs to be represented in the how-to-get-published literature – as it now will be with *How to Get Published and Make a Lot of Money.*

Book's Table of Contents

Introduction: You Can Become a Published Author

PART I: EXACTLY WHAT YOU NEED TO DO TO GET PUBLISHED IN THE ORDER IN WHICH YOU NEED TO DO IT – AND ALL YOU NEED TO KNOW ABOUT EACH STEP

1. Expunge All the Publishing Horror Stories You Have Ever Heard.
2. Establish a Clear Goal for Your Book.
3. Delineate Your Book's Original Contribution.
4. Start Working on a Fabulous Title.
5. Decide Whether You Are Going to Self-Publish or Sell to a Publisher.
6 (or 12). Write the Manuscript.
7. Write the Proposal.
8. Enlist a Famous or Highly-Credentialled Person to Write Your Preface.
9. Enlist the Services of a Fabulous Literary Agent.
10. Sell Your Book.
11. Negotiate and Sign Your Contract.
12. Write Your Book.
13. Revise Your Manuscript – And Keep Your Editor Happy.
14. Discuss Subsidiary Sales with Your Agent.
15. Solicit Endorsement Statements.
16. Plan Your Promotion and Publicity.
17. Celebrate Your Publication Date.
18. Be a Vigilant and Relentless Guardian Over the Fatal Gap.
19. Relax and Wait for Cheques to Arrive in Your Postbox.
20. Start Working on Your Next Book.

PART II – SUSAN PAGE'S EIGHT LAWS OF SUCCESS IN WRITING AND GETTING PUBLISHED

1. You Have to Believe You Will Succeed.
2. If You Want to Succeed, You Have to Begin.

3. You Can't Succeed Without Inner Commitment, But You Can't Force It Either.
4. Things Take Time.
5. The Fertile Void Is a Necessary Phase.
6. Inspiration Comes While You Are Working.
7. Everything You Do Is an Experiment.
8. Comparison Is the Basis of All Misery.

Chapter-by-Chapter Outline

Introduction

The Introduction will excite readers about their own chances of getting published and entice them to read on. It opens with two anecdotes about authors I assisted. For example, one woman took my advice (with great apprehension) to reject a £5,000 advance offer. But after I spent several hours with her and she followed my suggestions, she received a £55,000 offer. The advice I gave her over lunch is the same information I am about to present in this book.

The Introduction will demonstrate that accurate information is hard to come by – for example, what I consider to be the three most important steps are never even mentioned in one popular publishing guide – and will explain how I learned what to do and why I don't believe the whole process should continue to be shrouded in mystery.

Finally, the Introduction will explain that the book is designed for writers at every level, both fiction and non-fiction, and that all writers – no matter what the current status of their manuscript – will benefit most by beginning with Step 1 and following the steps in order.

PART I – EXACTLY WHAT YOU NEED TO DO TO GET PUBLISHED IN THE ORDER IN WHICH YOU NEED TO DO IT – AND ALL YOU NEED TO KNOW ABOUT EACH STEP

Step 1: Expunge All the Publishing Horror Stories You Have Ever Heard

Chapter One offers – with humour – a succinct catalogue of all that writers dislike about the publishing industry and all the awful things that they have heard can happen. So, it continues, the question is *not* are the cards stacked against you. They are. The question is are you going to let this defeat you, or are you going to take it as all the more reason to become systematic and persevering in your effort to get published? The latter is the only appropriate option. Don't let these stories surprise and upset you any more. Be prepared for them. Arm yourself for the inevitable. You can join groups that are trying to make changes in the publishing industry, but don't wait around for them to succeed.

This chapter will limit itself to *relevant* information about the publishing industry, presented so that readers know exactly how to use it.

2. Establish a Clear Goal for Your Book

Knowing exactly *why* you are writing your book is crucial because your goal will influence important decisions every step of the way. Having a clear goal will keep you motivated and be a rudder for you when the seas get stormy.

Why are you writing this book? For example:
I have a burning desire to share these ideas.
I love to write and want to be rewarded for it.
I need a product. I need something to sell at my speeches.
I want this book to position me in the marketplace, to open business opportunities for me.
I want to make money. (Be specific: how much money?)

What is your fondest hope for the book? Exactly what outcomes would you consider to be moderately or extremely successful?

Chapter Two will cover:

- the importance of written goals in general
- factors that affect the size of a royalty advance
- the common mistake of setting a goal that is inappropriately low
- the crucial, little-known skill of keeping hopes high and expectations realistic
- an actual step-by-step procedure for setting a goal and writing it down

3. Delineate Your Book's Original Contribution

Write a sentence or short paragraph stating three things:

1. Why there is a need for your book.
2. How your book will fill that need.
3. How your book is distinctive from every other book in the world.

To be successful, a book must make an original contribution, it must be distinctive. It won't necessarily have brand-new content. It can be distinctive in its presentation, in its vocabulary, in its imagery – but it must contribute something new.

Using numerous examples, Chapter Three will make a strong case for spending time on this step early in the writing or proposal process and then returning to reassess it often, for as the project evolves, its distinctive contribution may shift or become more obvious.

4. Start Working on a Fabulous Title

A wonderful, special title can add enormous energy and focus to a book project. Sometimes coming up with the perfect title is very difficult. It is one part of the process over which you have less control, for you are totally dependent upon inspiration. Get the process of title-searching started early and keep working on it all along.

Chapter Four contains:

- seven clever, effective methods for stimulating intuition, actual exercises to help a writer find a brilliant title
- characteristics of a good title
- title styles
- numerous examples

5. Decide Whether You Are Going to Self-Publish or Sell to a Publisher

Don't rush ahead with trying to sell a book to a publisher without some understanding of the self-publishing option. There are many popular misconceptions about it. Take time to look at least briefly at both possibilities.

Most people think the disadvantages of self-publishing are these:

1. You have to do your own publicity.
2. You have to do your own distribution and it won't be as good.
3. You won't make as much money.
4. It is not as prestigious.

In fact, all of these could be the results of selling to an established publisher and might not be true of self-publishing – and large sums of money can be made or sacrificed using either method.

The important differences between the two paths are actually these: When you self-publish, you have to start with some of your own money, and you have to do your own work.

Chapter Five continues with a thorough but precise discussion of the pros and cons of each route and includes questionnaires to help readers determine the best route for them.

Readers who determine that self-publishing makes more sense for them are referred to other resources, for this book is not a guide to self-publishing.

6 (or 12). Write the Manuscript

Here, for the first time, the order of these steps becomes optional. Some writers will write part or all of their manuscript before trying to sell it. Others will write the proposal first and hope to be paid to write the book. The pros and cons of each of these options will be discussed.

Chapter Six also covers:

- basic writing and research skills
- ways to get started writing a book
- methods for organising material and for generating organisational schemes
- the wise use of editors and writing consultants
- using ghostwriters
- collaborating

7. Write the Proposal

Chapter Seven takes the mystery – and fear – out of writing a book proposal. Whether or not your manuscript is complete, writing your proposal will strengthen your final book because it will force you to tighten your organisation and refine your ideas.

Chapter Seven reveals 'Susan Page's Distinctive, Proven Formula for a Stunning Book Proposal – Fiction or Non-fiction.' This 'programme' goes far beyond listing the components of the proposal; it show writers exactly how to move through each step. Everything a person needs to know to write a winning proposal is here – and nothing else.

8. Enlist a Famous or Highly Credentialled Person to Write Your Preface

This step is optional, and the reasons for and against doing it will be discussed.

There is one important secret to getting someone big and important to write you a preface: Ask! If you know anyone or know anyone who knows anyone, use your connections. But if you don't, ask anyway.

This step can take place later too, especially if the manuscript is not yet written. But if you can get a famous name behind you before you begin to approach agents, it will make that task easier.

Again, a specific formula for approaching famous people will be presented with sample letters and phone conversations and amusing, educational anecdotes.

9. Enlist the Services of a Fabulous Literary Agent

During the six years I was trying to figure out how to proceed with my book idea, I must have asked one hundred supposedly knowledgeable people why I should consider using an agent. I now know of seven powerful, compelling reasons, but in six years, I never received a satisfactory answer to my question. Some people felt it was a good idea, some felt it was a waste of money, but no one ever told me why.

Furthermore, I could never get genuinely helpful information on how to select or acquire an agent or how to know whether I had a 'good' one. 'Ask around,' people would tell me. 'Network.' And all books ever said was, 'Look in the *Literary Market Place.'*

Here at last is the 'rap' on agents that I wish someone had given me six years ago before I was lucky enough to blunder into a good (indeed, extraordinary) agent.

Chapter Nine offers:

- seven compelling reasons why it makes sense to use an agent and is foolish to proceed without one
- exactly what characteristics to insist upon in an agent and how to determine whether a given agent has them
- six specific, effective methods for finding good agents
- a step-by-step guide for approaching agents that incorporates all of agents' popular likes and dislikes
- what to do when an agent selects you
- the agent's contract

10. Sell Your Book

If you have properly completed Steps 1 to 9, Step 10 consists of two parts:

1. Wait for the phone to ring, and
2. Order the champagne.

Chapter Ten explains what authors need to know about how sales or auctions take place, and offers several upbeat anecdotes about first-time authors selling books. The chapter makes the following points:

1. Appropriate expectations make all the difference in your book sale experience.
2. It is important to mark the sale of your first book with some kind of celebration.

11. Negotiate and Sign Your Contract

It will take you about one full day to become a mini-expert on publishing contracts. Though you should let your agent negotiate your contract, I strongly urge you to become familiar with all the clauses and especially the most common controversial issues, and to be sure your agent knows what you consider to be important. Publishing contracts are actually quite interesting, and understanding them will make you a wiser, more savvy author. It is well worth the few hours it takes!

Chapter Eleven offers readers two resources and explains how best to use one day to evaluate their own contract and to become knowledgeable about publishing contracts in general. It includes a discussion of the most common controversies, and organisations that are working to make contracts more author-oriented.

Note to the Reader: Chapters Twelve to Twenty were described in similar detail in the actual proposal I submitted to publishers.

PART II – SUSAN PAGE'S EIGHT LAWS OF SUCCESS IN WRITING AND GETTING PUBLISHED

Section Two describes the psychological and motivational factors that keep writers from becoming authors. It helps enormously to know exactly what to do to get published and how to proceed (Section I). But equally important is to be prepared for the debilitating behavioural patterns and emotions that are almost bound to emerge during the process – and to know how to get through them.

Susan Page has collected these principles over the last thirteen years of her own development as a writer and speaker. She has presented parts of this material in lectures, but here for the first time, she gathers all her wisdom together in the form of Eight Laws that she believes govern the creative process. She knows from all the counselling she has done with authors-in-progress that most people blame themselves when they feel stuck and don't know enough about the creative process to anticipate that it can sometimes be painful.

Each of the following laws will be elucidated in two to five pages of inspiring, motivational, sometimes humorous explanations and anecdotes.

1. You have to believe you will succeed.
2. If you want to succeed, you have to begin.
3. You can't succeed without inner commitment, but you can't force it either.
4. Things take time.
5. The fertile void is a necessary phase.
6. Inspiration comes while you are working.
7. Everything you do is an experiment.
8. Comparison is the basis of all misery.

Resources

I have deliberately refrained from inundating you with unnecessary 'resources' that will tempt you to waste time you could be using to write. I have included only resources to which I have made reference in the Twenty Steps and a few others I feel might be genuinely useful.

WRITERS' CONFERENCES

Arvon Foundation (five-day residential courses offering writers the chance to live and work with professional writers)
Contact: Totleigh Barton, Sheepwash, Beaworthy, Devon EX21 5NS
Tel: 01409 231338
Lumb Bank, Heptonstall, Hebden Bridge, West Yorkshire HX7 6DF
Tel: 01422 843714
Moniack Mhor, Teavarran, Kiltarlity, Beauly, Inverness-shire IV4 7HT
Tel: 01463 741675

Writers' Summer School, Swanwick (annual week-long summer school for everyone from beginners to published authors)
Contact: The Secretary, The New Vicarage, Parson's Street, Woodford Halse, Daventry, Northamptonshire NN11 3RE
Tel: 01327 261477

University of Southampton Annual Writers' Conference (the largest writers' conference in the UK)
Contact: Conference Organizer, Department of Adult Continuing Education, University of Southampton, Southampton, Hampshire SO17 1BJ
Tel: 01703 593469

WRITERS' COURSES AND WORKSHOPS

Directory of Writers' Circles (contains contact addresses for more than 600 writers' groups nationwide)
Contact: Oldacre, Horderns Park Road, Chapel-en-le-Frith, High Peak SK23 9SY
Tel: 01298 812305

Scribo (circulates published and unpublished MSS in folio form to members for forum discussion)
Contact: Flat 1, 31 Hamilton Road, Boscombe, Bournemouth, Dorset BH1 4EQ
Tel: 01202 302533

Workers' Educational Association (WEA – runs writing courses and workshops throughout the country; details of regional courses available from head office)
Contact: Temple House, 17 Victoria Park Square, London E2 9PB
Tel: 0181 983 1515

PROFESSIONAL ASSOCIATIONS AND SOCIETIES

Association of Authors' Agents
Contact: Sheil Land Associates Ltd, 43 Doughty Street, London WC1N 2LF
Tel: 0171 405 9351

Author-Publisher Network
Contact: 12 Mercers, Hawkhurst, Kent TN18 4LH
Tel: 01580 753346

Book Trust (offers a free book information service)
Contact: Book House, 45 East Hill, London SW18 2QZ
Tel: 0181 870 9055

Professional Authors' and Publishers' Association (PAPA)
Contact: 292 Kennington Road, London SE11 4LD
Tel: 0171 582 1477

Society of Authors
Contact: 84 Drayton Gardens, London SW10 9SB
Tel: 0171 373 6642

The Society of Freelance Editors and Proofreaders
Contact: Mermaid House, 1 Mermaid Court, London SE1 1HR
Tel: 0171 403 5141

The Society of Indexers
Contact: Mermaid House, 1 Mermaid Court, London SE1 1HR
Tel: 0171 403 4947

Writers' Guild of Great Britain
Contact: 430 Edgware Road, London W2 1EH
Tel: 0171 723 8074

PUBLICATIONS

The Bookseller
Contact: 12 Dyott Street, London WC1A 1DF
Tel: 0171 420 6000

The New Writer
Contact: PO Box 60, Cranbrook, Kent TN17 2ZR
Tel: 01580 212626

Writers' Monthly
Contact: 235–239 High Road, London N22 4HF
Tel: 0181 365 8101

Writers' News (available to members only)
Contact: PO Box 4, Nairn, Highland IV12 4HU

Writing (available from some newsagents)
Contact: PO Box 4, Nairn, Highland IV12 4HU

BOOKS

Guide to Literary Prizes, Grants and Awards in Britain and Ireland
(available from Book Trust)
Writers' and Artists' Yearbook (A & C Black, annual)
The Writers' Handbook (Macmillan, annual)

Index